ORIGAMI
ANIMAL FRIENDS

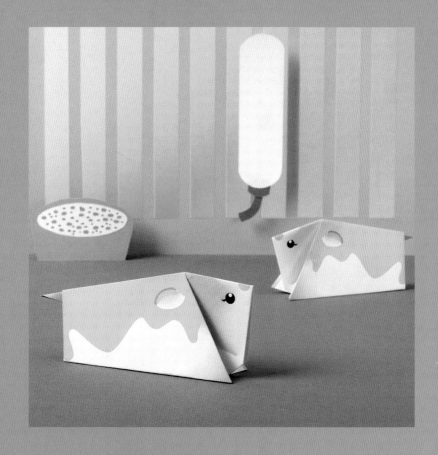

ORIGAMI
ANIMAL FRIENDS

Fold **35** of your favorite cats,
dogs, rabbits, and more

MARI ONO

CICO BOOKS
LONDON NEW YORK

Published in 2017 by CICO Books
An imprint of Ryland Peters & Small Ltd

20–21 Jockey's Fields
London WC1R 4BW

341 E 116th St
New York, NY 10029

www.rylandpeters.com

10 9 8 7 6 5 4 3

Text © Mari Ono 2017
Design, illustration, and photography © CICO Books 2017

A CIP catalog record for this book
is available from the Library of
Congress and the British Library.

ISBN: 978 1 78249 422 5

Printed in China

Editor: Robin Gurdon
Designer: Jerry Goldie
Photographer: Geoff Dann
Stylist: Trina Dalziel
Origami paper illustrator: Takumasa Ono

CONTENTS

Introduction 6

Part One
IN THE HOUSE

1 **Inu** Dog 10

2 **Bokuyo-Ken** Sheepdog 12

3 **Dacksfund** Dachshund 16

4 **Terria** Scottish Terrier 20

5 **Himalayan Neko** Himalayan Cat 24

6 **Perushia Neko** Persian Cat 28

7 **Tora Neko** Tabby Cat 32

8 **Ko Inu** Puppy 34

9 **Ko Neko** Kitten 38

10 **Kinuge Nezumi** Hamster 40

11 **Kingyo** Goldfish 42

Part Two
IN THE GARDEN

12 **Tento Mushi** Ladybug 48

13 **Semi** Cicada 50

14 **Kaeru** Frog 52

15 **Hari Nezumi** Hedgehog 54

16 **Hastuka Nezumi** Mouse 56

17 **Kabuto Mushi** Japanese Rhinoceros Beetle 60

18 **Katatsumuri** Snail 62

19 **Hato** Pigeon 64

20 **Kujyaku** Peacock 66

Part Three
ON THE FARM

21 **Buta** Pig 70

22 **Usagi** Rabbit 74

23 **Taremimi Usagi** Hopping Rabbit 78

24 **Ahiru** Duck 82

25 **Itachi** Ferret 86

26 **Niwatori** Chicken 90

27 **Uma** Horse 94

Part Four
IN THE WILD

28 **Sekisei Inko** Parakeet 100

29 **Oumu** Parrot 102

30 **Nihon Zaru** Monkey 104

31 **Hebi** Snake 108

32 **Tokage** Lizard 112

33 **Yadokari** Hermit Crab 116

34 **Netaigyo** Angel Fish 120

35 **Fugu** Blowfish 124

Useful Information 126

Index 127

Acknowledgments 128

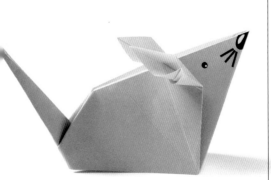

INTRODUCTION

From the very first time you attempt *origami* you will discover the magic that comes from turning a flat, two-dimensional piece of paper into a three-dimensional object with just a few simple folds. Now well known throughout the world, *origami* began in Japan as one of the country's traditional arts and developed throughout the nation's long history. One of the earliest references to *origami* was written by nobles in the Heian period of the 10th and 11th century describing how to fold a "frog." Later, in the Edo period, which prospered for more than 200 years between 1603 and 1868, a variety of *origami* models were created and these are now the basis for the designs that are still in use today. As each generation passes on the knowledge to their children and grandchildren *origami* has continued to be a vital part of traditional learning.

This "culture of folding paper" was closely related to the art of preparing washcloths or tea towels—*tenugui*—and traditional Japanese wrapping cloths—*furoshiki*. All were part of the Japanese "wrapping culture," which developed in the Muromachi era in the 14th century. The custom demonstrated cordiality and respect to a person being presented with a gift by using creatively folded wrapping paper. Such a courteous way of using paper was then developed into the more practical *origami* art, and became one of the *omotenashi* (Japanese spirit of hospitality) arts in modern Japan.

Using our fingers to practice *origami* stimulates the brain and improves concentration, as well as promoting creativity. It helps children's brain development and expands their education in a way which can't be replicated by playing video games. For the adult brain, it has been proven in the fields of medicine and care for the elderly that *origami* exercises the brain and can be used for healing.

This book includes designs for a variety of cute animals, all created with *origami* and which are full of uniqueness. I hope not only children but also adults can enjoy them together. Start with a simple model first using some basic folds such as *sikaku ori* (square fold) *sankaku ori* (triangle fold), *zabuton ori* (cushion fold) and *tako ori* (kite fold). Learning these simple folds will help you to develop your *origami* skills and be ready for more complicated designs.

The feeling of achievement that you can get from accomplishing more difficult models will allow you to feel the pleasure of *origami* folding. I hope that this book will give as many people as possible the experience of enjoyment from *origami*, so now's the time to get started and enjoy!

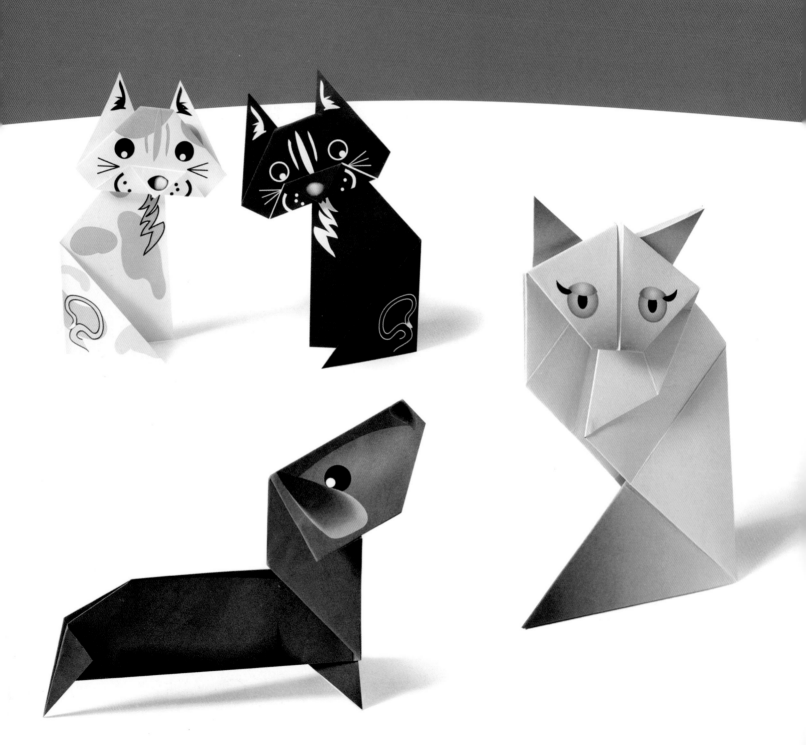

1 INU DOG

Making a lovely, large-eared dog is extremely simple. You can use large pieces of paper and then turn them into masks to wear and play with. When you have folded the face, draw on the dog's features and whiskers. Don't worry about accuracy; any kind of face will give your dog character. Try using different colored paper for different breeds.

You will need:
1 sheet of 6 in (15 cm) square paper
Marker pen or stick-on craft eyes

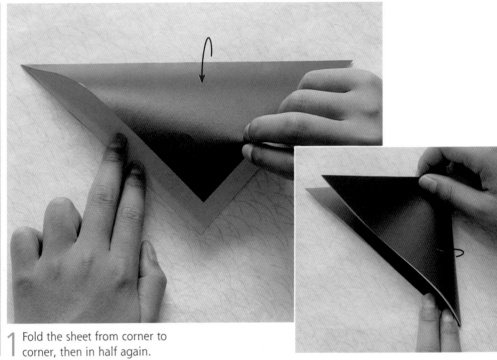

1 Fold the sheet from corner to corner, then in half again.

2 Open out the last fold and turn down the corners to make the ears.

3 Turn the object over and fold the top forward to make a flat edge.

4 Turn the object back over and fold up the front sheet of the bottom flap before turning the tip of the folded flap back over.

10

IN THE HOUSE

5 Fold up the back flap and tuck it inside the object. Draw or stick on the eyes.

2 BOKUYO-KEN SHEEPDOG

The sheepdog, or border collie, is widely regarded as one of the most intelligent and obedient dog breeds. It is a very easy animal to train, which is why the sheepdog is a farmer's best friend and closest colleague as he races around the fields to his master's whistled commands, shepherding the sheep into their pen as if by magic.

You will need:
1 sheet of 6 in (15 cm) square paper
Scissors

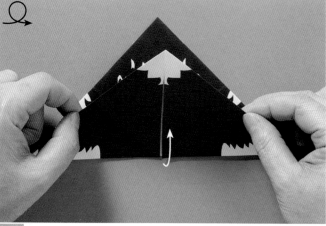

1 Fold the sheet in half from corner to corner to make a crease, opening out each time, then fold the corners in to meet in the center. Turn the paper over and fold in half.

13

2 Lift the top flap, open it out, and press the corner to sit on the top point, making a square fold. Turn the object over and repeat so you are left with a diamond shape.

3 Fold down the upper part of the top flap to make a crease line between the two outer points.

4 Open out the top flap and press flat into a rectangular shape so that the vertical edges now run horizontally.

5 Turn the paper over and repeat, then fold the upper flap on the left-hand side to the right. Turn the paper over again and repeat.

6 Fold the upper flaps in so that their edges meet along the central crease, then turn the paper over and repeat.

7 Fold the right-hand flap to the left, turn the paper over, and repeat.

8 Fold over the left-hand point at an angle to make a crease, then open up the left-hand side of the paper and refold the flap inside to form the head.

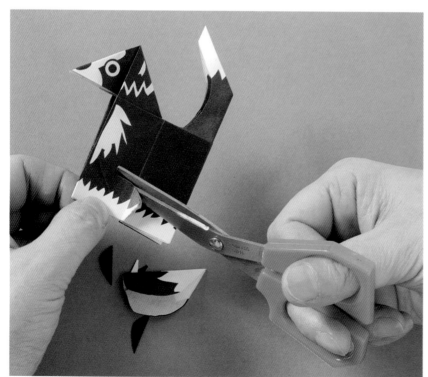

9 Use the pair of scissors to cut out the shape of the tail, then cut out the shape of the sheepdog's legs.

3 DACKSFUND DACHSHUND

The dachshund is commonly known as the sausage dog. It is famous for its short legs and long body, which wobbles as it moves, and is loved as a pet dog by people all over the world. This *origami* model recreates the dog's extraordinary shape. Take care when you adjust the body shape by folding it in half—as the model has many layers, you must make firm creases to finish it off beautifully.

You will need:
1 sheet of 6 in (15 cm) square paper

IN THE HOUSE

1 With the design side facing down, fold the paper in half from corner to corner both ways, opening out each time, then fold the side points in so that they meet at the center. Now fold the sides in again so that they also meet along the center line.

2 Open out the paper and fold over the left-hand side, using the crease line to the left of the center line.

3 Turn back the lower edge of the flap so that it runs along the left-hand vertical edge, then fold over the upper edge in the same way.

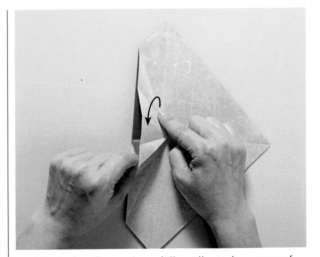

4 Lift the last flap and carefully pull out the corner of paper, folding it down the side of the object, reversing the direction of the diagonal crease, and flattening it again to form a triangle.

5 Fold over the newly formed point to the left so that the folded edge now runs horizontally. Lift the flap and carefully refold the point inside, reversing the direction of the creases where necessary.

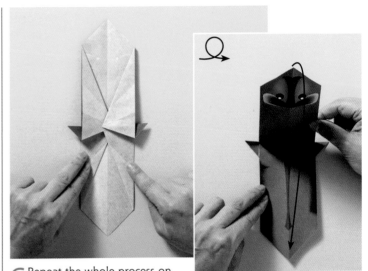

6 Repeat the whole process on the other side, then turn the model over and fold back the head to form a new crease, in line with the straight edges of the two small flaps.

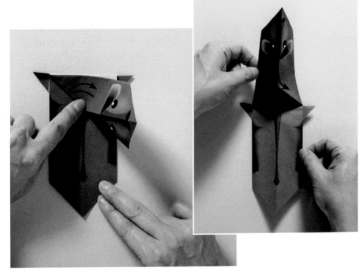

7 Turn the top flap over to the right so that the left edge now runs across the top of the object and press down a crease only as far as the center line. Open and repeat by folding the top flap to the left. Lift up the tip and press it down so that the base forms a triangle.

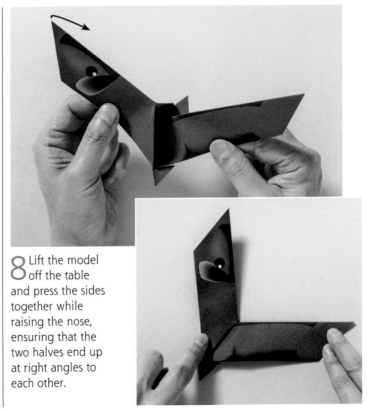

8 Lift the model off the table and press the sides together while raising the nose, ensuring that the two halves end up at right angles to each other.

10 Open up the neck again and fold it to the left so that the creases made in the previous step form the shape of the head surrounding the neck.

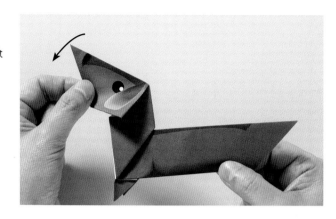

9 Fold down the head so that the tip of the nose touches the horizontal base of the model and form a crease. Release and fold the head back to form a second, angled crease starting from the same point on the right-hand edge of the neck.

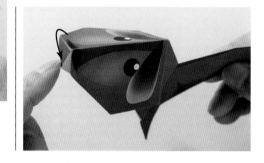

11 Turn over the tip to form a flat nose, folding it inside the face.

12 Fold over the right-hand end of the model at an angle to form a crease, then carefully open out the model, refolding the tip inside and reversing the direction of the creases where necessary.

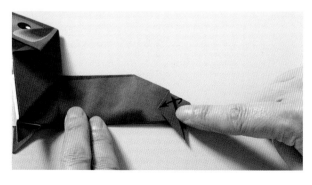

13 To finish, fold forward the right-hand points to form the straight edges of the dog's back legs.

4 TERRIA
SCOTTISH TERRIER

Now popular as a pretty pet dog, the Scottie has a long history as a hunting dog. Although small, it is always brave and will stop at nothing to catch its prey. When making the model it can be difficult to fold the head into shape because you are changing the direction of some of the creases. Always ask an adult for help if you have trouble.

You will need:
1 sheet of 6 in (15 cm) square paper

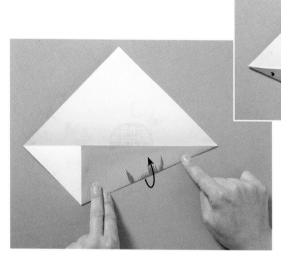

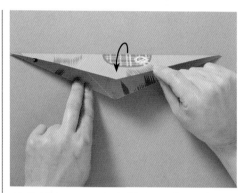

1 With the design side facing down, fold the paper in half from corner to corner through the design, then open out and fold in the two right-hand edges so that they meet along the central crease. Next, turn the two remaining edges over in the same way.

2 Fold the paper in half along the central crease.

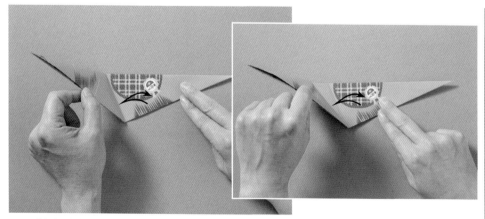

3 Fold the left-hand point over at an angle, using the edge of the flaps inside as a guide, to make a crease. Open out again and make a second crease, from the bottom point across the end of the dotted line shown on the design.

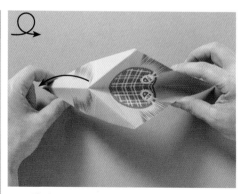

4 Lift the paper and turn it over. Pinch the right-hand side together and fold over the left-hand end, using the creases just made to surround the right-hand end and reversing the direction of the creases where necessary.

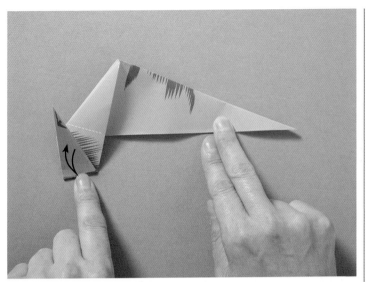

5 Turn over the bottom tip at an angle, using the dotted line on the design as a guide.

6 Next, open up the bottom flap and turn the tip back up so that it surrounds the flap.

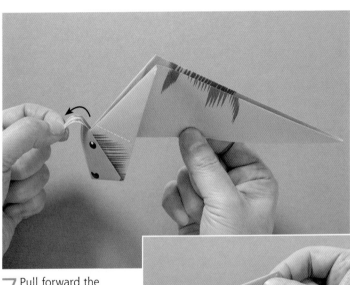

7 Pull forward the corner of paper that now sits above the neck to form the ears, then press the whole head back, creasing the paper along the dotted line shown on the design across the neck.

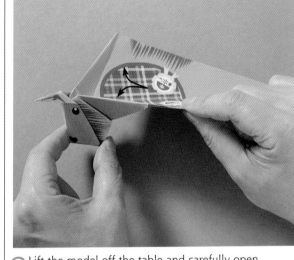

8 Lift the model off the table and carefully open up the back before closing it again in the other direction, with the head again surrounding the body.

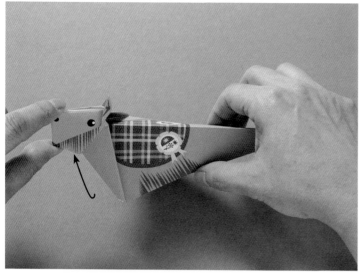

9 Now carefully push the head up, using the second crease made in Step 3.

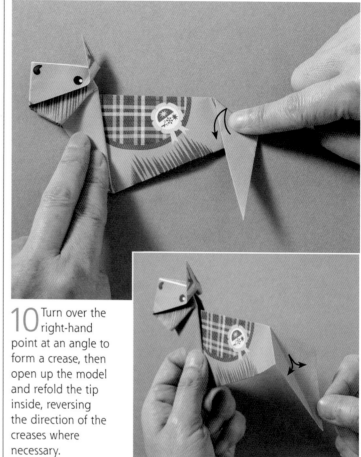

10 Turn over the right-hand point at an angle to form a crease, then open up the model and refold the tip inside, reversing the direction of the creases where necessary.

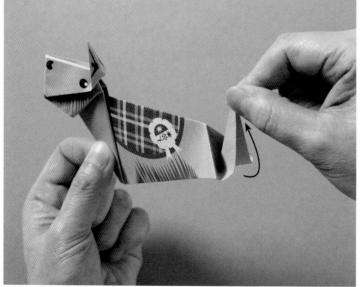

11 To finish fold up the same point once more inside the model to form the tail, ensuring the crease is made above the bottom edge of the model.

5 HIMALAYAN NEKO
HIMALAYAN CAT

Himalayan cats, which were bred by crossing the Persian with the Siamese, are famous for their calm characteristics, which makes them extremely popular as pets. You can change the expression on the model's face depending on how you fold the nose and ears—see the difference between a happy and sad cat just by reshaping its face.

You will need:
1 sheet of 6 in (15 cm) square paper

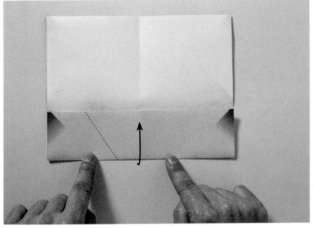

1 With the design side facing down, fold the paper in half from side to side both ways, opening out each time, to make creases, and then fold the bottom and top edges in to meet along the center line.

2 Fold in both sides so that they also meet in the middle of the paper.

3 Open out the flaps just made and fold the corners in at an angle so that the sides now run along the center line.

IN THE HOUSE

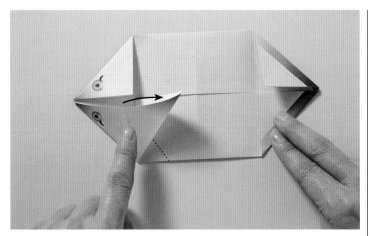

4 Carefully lift each flap and pull up the corner of paper, turning it along the center of the model and refolding it to form a triangle.

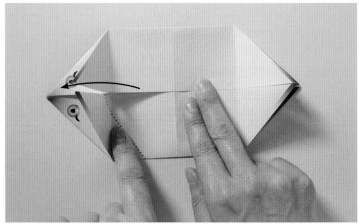

5 Fold all the newly made corners of the triangular flaps back to the points at the far sides of the model.

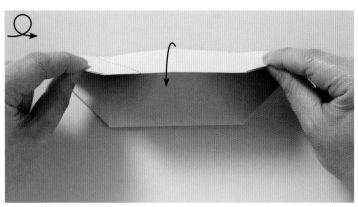

6 Turn the paper over and fold the model in half along the central crease.

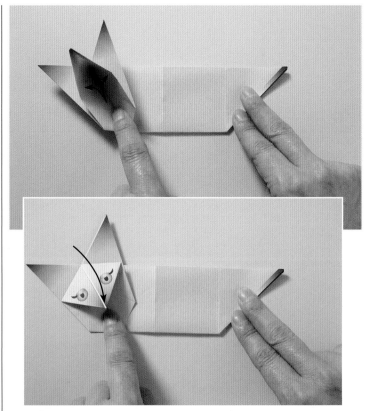

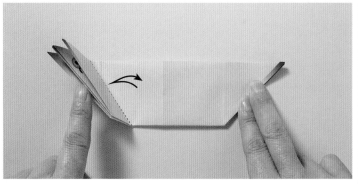

7 Fold over the left-hand end of the model at an angle using the dotted line on the design as a guide.

8 Open up the top sheet of this new flap, turning it back to the left to reveal the cat's face. Pull forward the tip inside and flatten it, ensuring that the central lines of the face and the neck match up.

9 Carefully turn back the bottom point of the face to create the cat's nose.

10 Turn back the ears and then fold them forward again to make a concertina fold. Turn the model over to check that both ears are folded evenly.

11 With the model the right side up again, fold over the right-hand end at an angle, then open up the body and refold it inside, reversing the direction of the creases where necessary, to form the cat's tail.

6 PERUSHIA NEKO
PERSIAN CAT

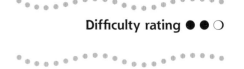

This Persian cat has a bit of an attitude—happily resting on a windowsill with a swanky look on her face and letting the world rush on around her. You can make her seem more or less at ease by subtly changing the size of the concertina fold that makes her neck and the angle at which you fold her tail at the end of the project.

You will need:
1 sheet of 6 in (15 cm) square paper

1 With the design side facing down, fold the paper in half from side to side both ways, opening out each time, to make creases, then fold the bottom and top edges in to meet along the center line. Fold in the left-hand end so that the edge runs down the center line.

2 Open out the last fold and turn both corners in so that they meet on the center line.

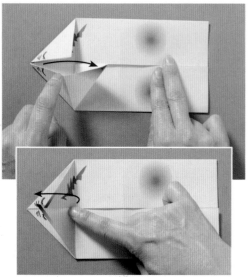

3 Carefully open up the flaps just made, each time lifting up the corner of paper from inside, and turn them along the center line to form a triangular flap. Fold the right-hand points of both flaps back to the left-hand point of the model.

4 Turn the paper over and fold the left-hand point over to the right, then turn back the flap to make a concertina fold.

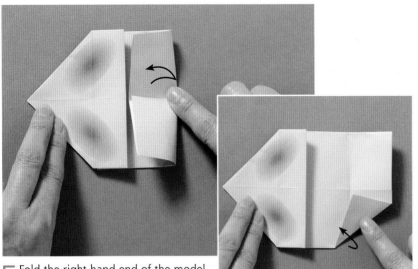

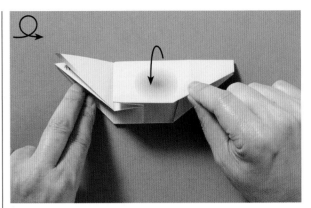

5 Fold the right-hand end of the model over to the edge of the concertina fold, taking care to make a crease only in the center as a marker. Open out the fold and turn the right-hand corners over at an angle so that they meet each other on the central crease at the mark just made.

6 Turn the model over and fold it in half along the central crease.

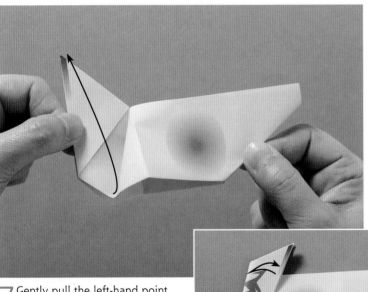

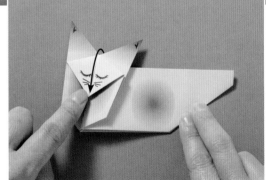

7 Gently pull the left-hand point out and upward, opening up the concertina fold and flattening it. Turn the left-hand end over at a slight angle from the bottom left-hand point, ensuring that all the design is visible.

8 Turn the top sheet of this new flap back to the left to reveal the cat's face. Open up the flap of paper inside and flatten it, ensuring that the central lines of the face and the neck match up.

9 Carefully turn back the bottom tip of the face to create the cat's nose.

10 Turn over the model and fold back the top points so that the creases match the shape of the head, then fold them back in concertina folds to make small ears.

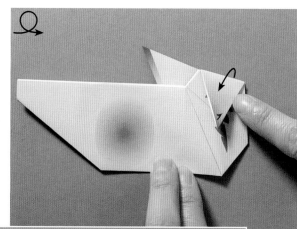

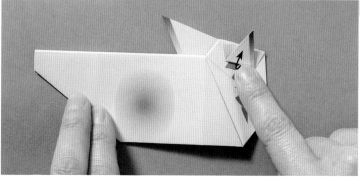

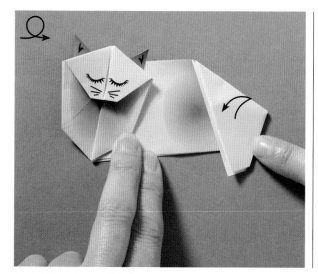

11 With the model the right side up again, fold over the right-hand end at an angle.

12 Open up the body and refold the flap inside, reversing the direction of the creases where necessary, then finish by turning the point back up to form the cat's tail.

7 TORA NEKO TABBY CAT

This *origami* cat is a design that everyone can easily make. Each cat will become a real character, just as soon as you draw on a pair of eyes, a nose, and a set of whiskers using a marker pen. Experiment with different patterned paper to resemble different breeds of cat. Try using orange paper for a ginger tom or stripes for a tabby cat, for example.

You will need:
1 sheet of 6 in (15 cm) square paper
Marker pen

1 Fold over the paper from corner to corner, open it out, and fold between the other corners.

2 Turn back the top of the triangle, making a fold about ¾ in (2 cm) from the tip.

3 Fold up the right-hand corner from the center crease at an angle so that it just covers the triangle made in the previous step.

32

IN THE HOUSE

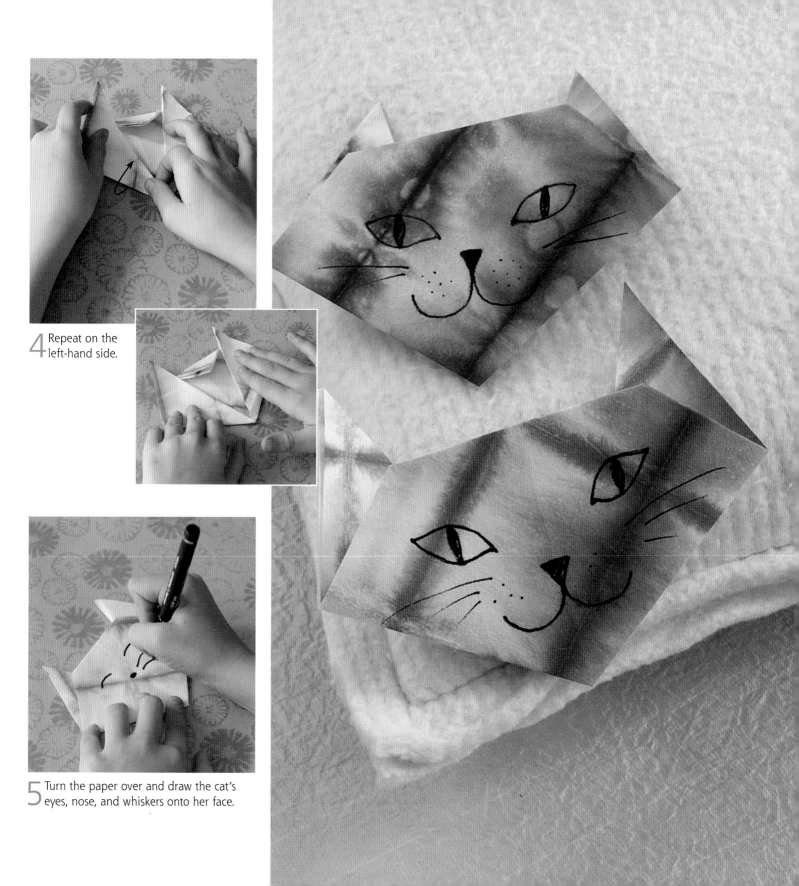

4 Repeat on the left-hand side.

5 Turn the paper over and draw the cat's eyes, nose, and whiskers onto her face.

8 KO INU PUPPY

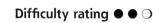
This pretty *origami* model of a puppy shows the sweet nature of the young dog but you will have to imagine just how rowdy and bouncy he is—at least with an *origami* model you will not have to spend hours playing with him and throwing his ball. Take care with this design as it starts in a unique way and you must ensure both sides are completely even to keep his face pretty.

You will need:
1 sheet of 6 in (15 cm) square paper

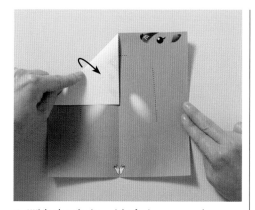

1 With the design side facing upward, fold the paper in half through the design and open out again, then fold down the top corners so that they meet along the central crease.

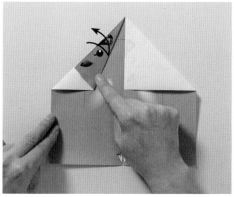

2 Fold the vertical edge of each of these flaps back over to the diagonal edge and make a crease.

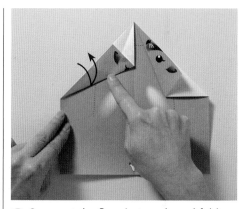

3 Open out the flaps just made and fold up the bottom edges, so that these now run along the diagonal edges.

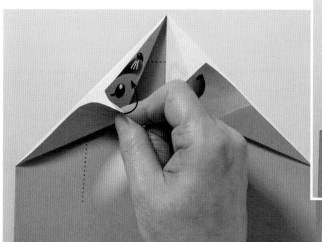

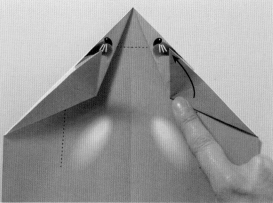

4 Lift up the whole flap on each side and pinch together the paper around the corner using the creases made in the last two steps. Press the main flap back down to the table and turn the folded corner over toward the top.

35

KO INU PUPPY

5 Turn the paper over and fold over the left-hand side of the paper so that the diagonal edge runs down the central crease. Repeat on the right-hand side, then fold up the bottom points so that the creases match the bottom edge.

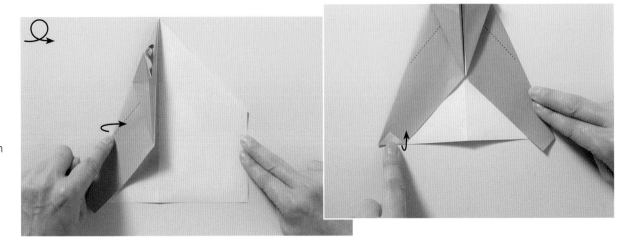

6 Fold up the bottom corner on the left-hand side so that the horizontal edge now runs up the central crease, tucking the corner under the flap to hold it in place. Repeat on the other side.

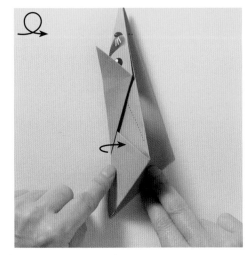

7 Turn the paper over and fold the model in half along the central crease.

8 Fold the top tip over to the left at an angle, following the dotted line on the design as a guide for the crease, and release.

9 Turn the paper over and place it back on the table as shown in the image. Carefully lift the flap made in the previous step and start pulling down the tip so that the inner surfaces open and become visible. Continue pulling down the tip so that the two sides of the flap begin to turn back and surround the main body of the model.

11 Fold over the bottom right-hand corner to make a diagonal crease, then release the flap and open up the body, pushing the tip of the flap up and around it to form the tail.

10 Fold the tip back underneath to form the puppy's snout.

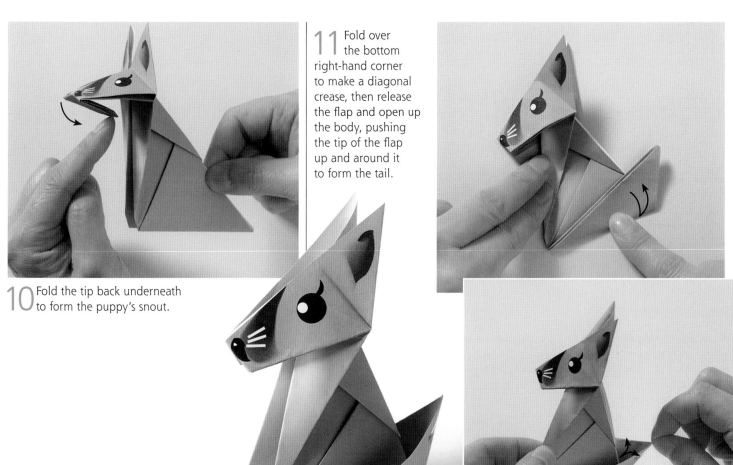

9 KO NEKO KITTEN

Difficulty rating ●●○

You will need:
1 sheet of 6 in (15 cm) square paper
Scissors

You can make two kittens from the paper supplied—one black, the other white. Cut each side of the paper in half again so that you can use one piece to make the head and the second to create the body. Remember to follow the design and fold the bodies in opposite directions so that they can face each other as they play.

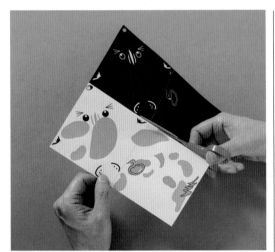

1 With the scissors, cut the paper in half and then cut each side in half again along the dotted line shown in the design.

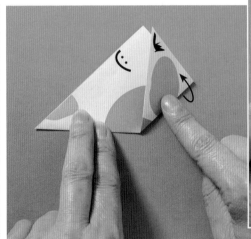

2 Take the small square of paper with the eyes and start forming the head by folding it in half from corner to corner. Fold the two outer points of this triangle up to the top point to form a diamond, then turn them back down at an angle, making fold lines from the outer points. Next fold up the bottom point.

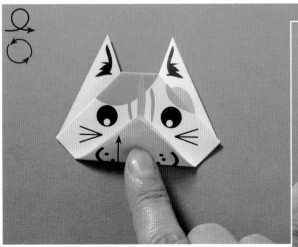

3 Turn the paper over and spin it through 180°. Fold up the bottom point, then turn it back, making a concertina fold between the whiskers shown on the design.

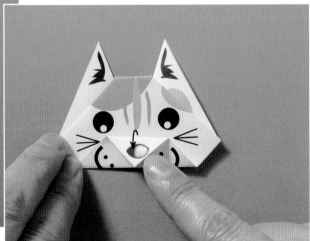

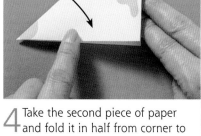

4 Take the second piece of paper and fold it in half from corner to corner, then fold the corner at the bottom of the diagonal fold over to the right-angled corner.

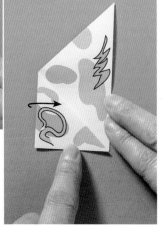

5 Pick up both pieces of paper and carefully slot the point at the top of the body into the opening at the back of the head.

10 KINUGE NEZUMI
HAMSTER

Hamsters are loved as small pets all over the world. They are the perfect animal for small children to look after as they race around their cages and run on their exercise wheel—that is, when they are not asleep in their beds. Hamsters have short tails so be careful not to leave too long a point when folding the tip back on itself in the second step.

Difficulty rating ● ● ○

You will need:
1 sheet of 6 in (15 cm) square paper

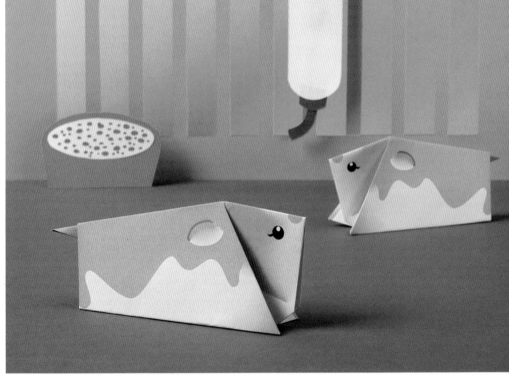

1 With the design side facing down, fold the paper in half through the design and open out, then turn the right-hand edges over so that they meet along the central crease. Fold the left-hand point over so that it touches the edges of the flaps.

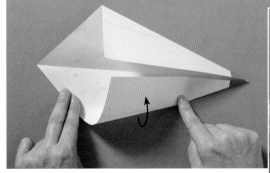

2 Fold the right-hand point over to the left edge, then turn it back so that it juts out beyond the edge of the paper and the lines on the design are aligned.

3 Fold the top and bottom edges over at an angle, using the dotted lines on the design as a guide.

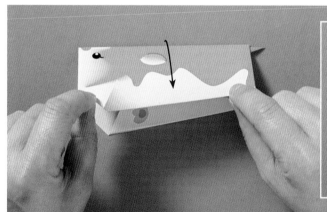

4 Fold the paper in half along the central crease, then fold the left-hand edge over at an angle, making a crease from the left-hand end of the bottom edge.

5 Open up the model and fold the left-hand end inside, using the creases just made and reversing them where necessary, then fold the point back out again, making a concertina fold. Ensure that all the features of the face are visible.

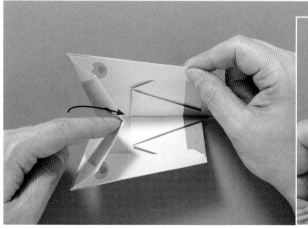
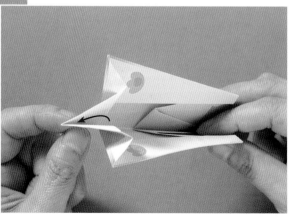

11 KINGYO GOLDFISH

This beautiful, waterdrop-pattern *origami* makes a goldfish that looks like it's swimming through dappled water.
The *kingyo* is one of origami's most magical designs from ancient times as, in the last step, it turns into a goldfish. It differs to many projects as you need to use scissors to finish it off, so make sure there is an adult around to help.

You will need:
1 sheet of 6 in (15 cm) square paper
Scissors

1 Fold the paper from corner to corner, then turn one of the outer corners up to the top point.

2 Repeat on the other corner and then turn the top flaps down to the bottom point.

3 Spin the paper 180° and turn the folded tips down and across at a 45° angle.

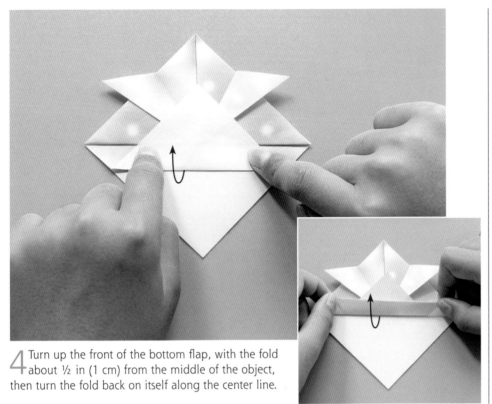

4 Turn up the front of the bottom flap, with the fold about ½ in (1 cm) from the middle of the object, then turn the fold back on itself along the center line.

5 Pick up the paper, turn it 90°, and use a small pair of scissors to cut ¾-in (2-cm) slits through the single layer of paper along the center line.

6 Fold the single layer of paper, that is left back behind the object.

7 Placing your fingers inside, pull open the object and flatten it down in the opposite direction.

8 Turn over the left-hand point to make a ½-in (1-cm) wide flap.

9 Let go of the flap and fold it back on itself, so that it ends inside the object.

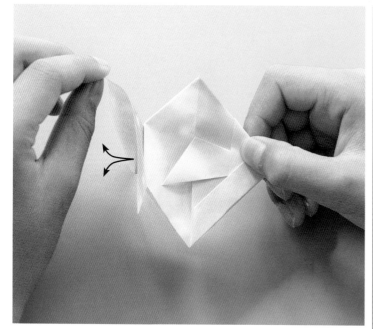

10 Pick up the object and fold out the flap on the left to make the goldfish's tail.

11 Finish by flattening out the tail so that it lies flush with the rest of the goldfish.

PART TWO
IN THE GARDEN

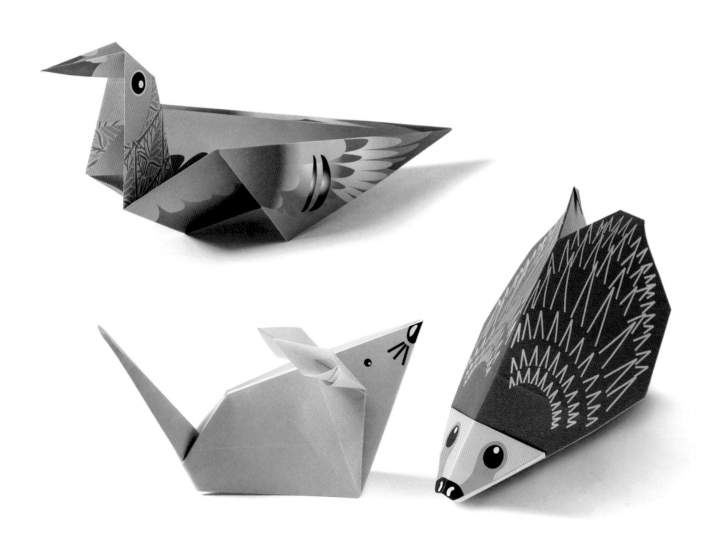

12 TENTO MUSHI LADYBUG

The spectacular ladybug is one of the most vivid insects in the forest, sometimes seen in large groups flying through the leaves and branches. Sadly, these *origami* ladybugs will never fly but you could use them as decoration near the window in your room, or put one on a greeting card to a friend. In addition, if you attach velour or felt and a pin to the reverse of the model, it can become a special *origami* brooch.

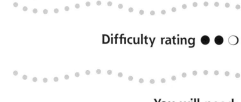

Difficulty rating ● ● ○

You will need:
1 sheet of 6 in (15 cm) square paper

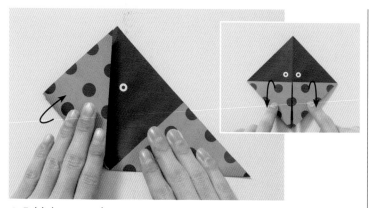

1 Fold the paper from corner to corner across the design, then turn the left and right points up to the top so that the bottom edges align up the middle of the paper. Fold down the upper tips, making creases across the middle of the model, to make a diamond shape.

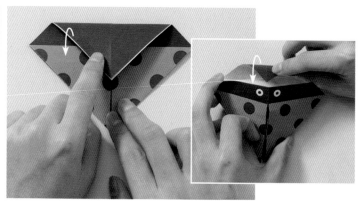

2 Turn down both parts of the top tip, making a new crease just above the eyes. Fold both flaps inside the design, reversing the crease of the front flap.

3 Turn the model over and fold in the two side points so that they meet at a slight angle in the center.

4 Open out the model and fold both flaps inside, reversing the creases. To finish, turn over the sides of the head at a slight angle.

13 SEMI CICADA

The cicada is an insect that has become famous as the traditional poetic symbol of the hot Japanese summer. Everybody can recall a day spent in the forest on holiday when they hear the cicada's cry during the heat. This model also resembles the traditional *origami* design for the helmet that was worn by the *samurai*. Because it is so very easy to make, even a small child will be able to master the challenge.

You will need:
1 sheet of 6 in (15 cm) square paper

1 With the design face down and the eyes at the top, fold the top of the sheet up from corner to corner, then fold both side points up to the top point so that the bottom edges align up the middle of the object.

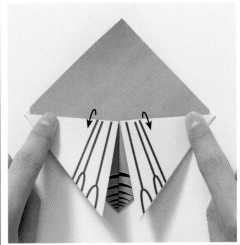

2 Turn down these flaps, making slightly angled fold lines from the outer points and ensuring the tips break out from the bottom edges of the object.

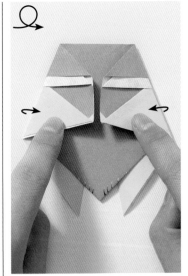

4 Turn the model over and fold in the side points at an angle so that the short edges meet along the center of the model.

3 Turn down the upper flap at the top, making a fold line about ½ in (1 cm) above the outer points, then fold over the remaining top flap to make a crease a further ⅛ in (0.25cm) above the center line.

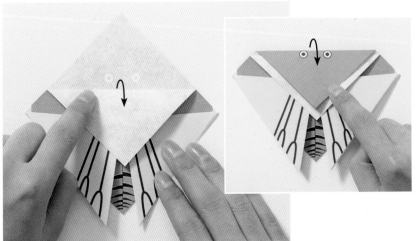

IN THE GARDEN

14 KAERU FROG

This little frog jumps when you push down lightly on its back legs with a finger. A simple design, you can make it with a group of friends, and have fun competing to see whose frog can jump the highest.

This is one of the most traditional *origami* models, dating from the days when there were not many toys for children to play with, and they had to make their own amusements.

• •

You will need:
1 sheet of 6 in (15 cm) square paper

1 Fold the paper in half, then open it out and repeat in the other direction before folding all the corners into the center.

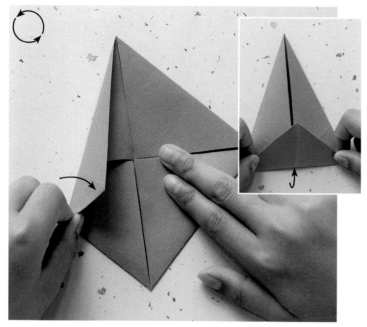

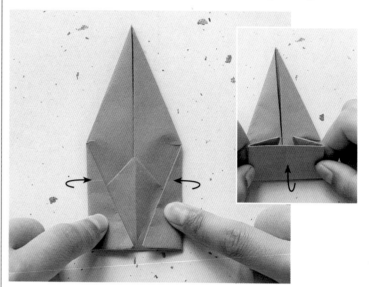

2 Spin the paper through 45°, turn in the outer points so that the edges run down the center line, and then fold up the bottom to make a triangle.

3 Turn in the bottom corners to the center line and fold the bottom up to the line where the corner flaps cross the lifted flap to make a crease.

4 Fold the flap made in Step 3 in half, bringing the end back down toward you.

5 Fold the tip forward to make the head and then let the object stand up. Push the back and watch it hop.

15 **HARI NEZUMI** HEDGEHOG

Supposedly named because so many hedgehogs were found under hedges, this prickly little animal lives in woods as well as gardens and is best known for curling up in a spiky ball when frightened so that it can evade predators. The *origami* model is easy to make with most of the fold lines matching the design.

You will need:
1 sheet of 6 in (15 cm) square paper

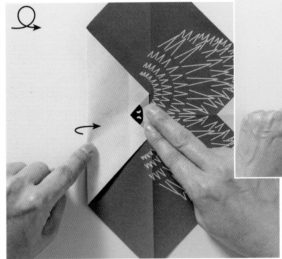

2 Turn the paper over and fold over the vertical edge to the central crease, then pull the tip across to the newly made edge.

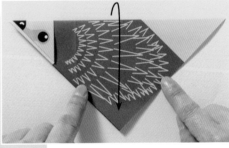

1 With the design side facing down, fold the paper in half from corner to corner both ways, opening out each time. Fold over the left-hand point, making a crease along the edge of the design, then open out again and refold the point up to the crease just made.

3 Turn the paper over and fold over the left-hand side so that the top and bottom of the vertical edge align along the horizontal central crease, then fold the model in half along the same crease.

IN THE GARDEN

4 Fold over the right-hand point at an angle, using the design to show the fold line, to make a crease, then open up the model and refold the point inside, reversing the direction of the creases where necessary.

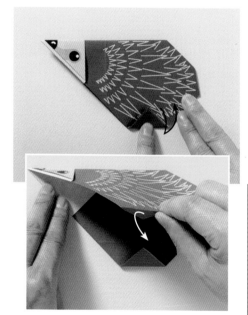

5 Fold both bottom points over to form a crease, then turn them over and tuck them inside the model to give it a horizontal base.

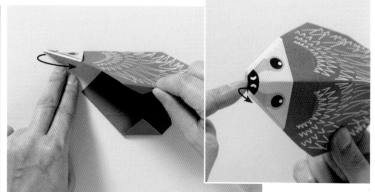

6 Finish by folding in the tip of the nose to form a snout.

16 HASTUKA NEZUMI MOUSE

Although the mouse is very friendly to people and has become one of the most popular animals to keep as a pet, we are not so happy if we find that one has sneaked into the house and is living behind a hole in the wall. Start with the diamond shape, one of the basic *origami* techniques, then straighten the tail and adjust the shape of the ears if you want to make him cuter.

Difficulty rating: ● ● ○

You will need:
1 sheet of 6 in (15 cm) square paper

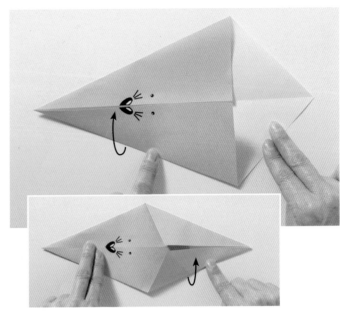

1 With the design side facing down, fold the paper in half from corner to corner through the design and open out, then fold the two left-hand edges in so that they meet along the central crease. Now fold over the right-hand sides in the same way.

2 Open up the top flap just made and lift the corner of paper out. Turn it across to the left and place it back on the center line, pressing it down to form a new triangular shaped flap. Repeat the process on the bottom flap.

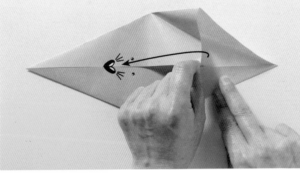

3 Turn the newly made flaps back to the right, then fold the diagonal edge of the top flap back to the left so that it runs down vertically from the top point.

4 Fold the upper flap to the left, then turn the flap's bottom point up over the horizontal edge of the flap.

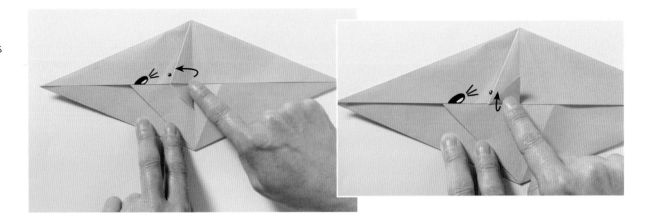

5 Repeat the last two steps on the lower flap.

6 Turn the paper over and fold over the left-hand point, making a crease just where the design of the nose becomes visible, then fold over the left-hand sides so that the vertical edges meet along the central crease.

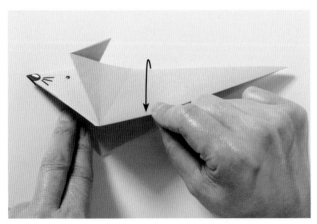

7 Fold the model in half along the central crease.

8 Fold the ears back, ensuring that the vertical edges now run along the top edge of the model, and making new diagonal creases.

9 Fold over the right-hand end at an angle to make a crease, then open up the model and refold the point inside, reversing the direction of the creases where necessary.

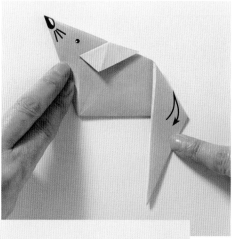

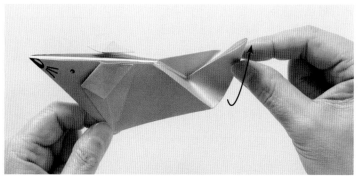

10 Fold the right-hand end back up, making the new creases as high up as possible inside the model.

11 Fold the back of the tail inside itself, running the edge along the crease in the middle of the tail, to give it a straight edge. Repeat on the other side of the tail.

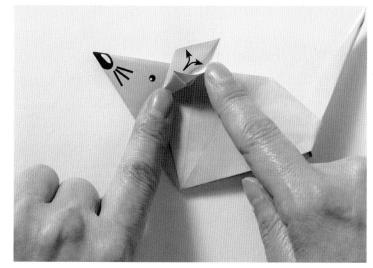

12 Finish by opening up the ears and pressing them flat.

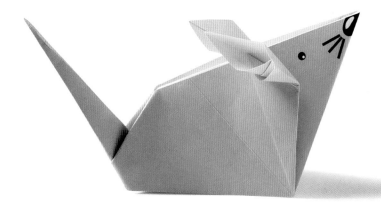

17 KABUTO MUSHI
JAPANESE RHINOCEROS BEETLE

Rhinoceros beetles are very popular in Japan. You can buy them at a pet store, but catching your own bugs in the forest is still one of the most popular summer traditions for Japanese children. After you have finished making the model and used the scissors to cut out the gap between the antennae, you can reset the central crease to give the beetle a more three-dimensional effect.

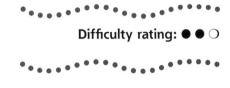

Difficulty rating: ● ● ○

You will need:
1 sheet of 6 in (15 cm) square paper
Scissors

IN THE GARDEN

1 With the design side facing down fold the paper in half through the design, then lift the right-hand end and refold it to the bottom point while opening out the flap and refolding it into a diamond shape. Repeat on the other side, then fold in the lower edges of the diamond to meet on the center line and fold down the top point over these flaps to make a crease.

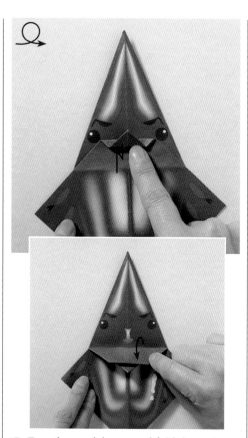

2 Release the triangle at the top, then open out the upper flaps, lifting the top sheet and folding it over to the top of the model, refolding the edges of the paper so that they meet along the center line.

3 Turn the model over and fold down the central triangle before folding it back over the crease you have just made in a concertina fold. Then turn the whole flap down toward the bottom of the model.

4 Turn the model back over and fold the top point to the right so that the diagonal edge runs horizontally and make a crease. Release and repeat to the right, then press the two sides of the long point together and push down toward the model's body, forming a triangular well.

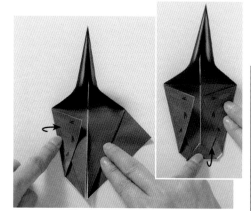

5 Fold in the two outer points at an angle and then fold up the bottom point.

6 Use the scissors to cut down the center of the long point and gently prise the two sides apart. Finish by emphasizing the diagonal creases across the center of the model to form the beetle's neck.

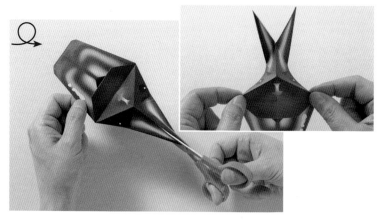

18 **KATATSUMURI** SNAIL

Snails have a terrible reputation for being slimy and slow as they leave their trails behind them when they cross the garden path, but they can be very beautiful with delicately patterned, spiraling shells. Even the smallest child can make this easy model by following the pictures, though they should always ask an adult for help with the scissors at the end.

Difficulty rating: ● ○ ○

You will need:
1 sheet of 6 in (15 cm) square paper
Scissors
Pencil

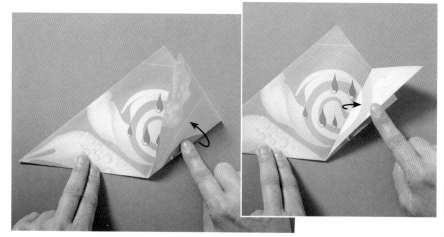

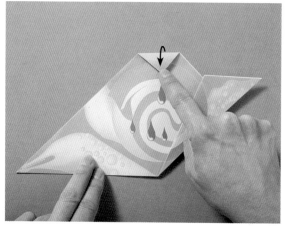

1 With the design side facing down, fold the paper in half through the design from corner to corner, then fold the right-hand point up to the top of the paper before turning it back so that its edge runs along the diagonal crease just made.

2 Fold down the top point to create a horizontal edge.

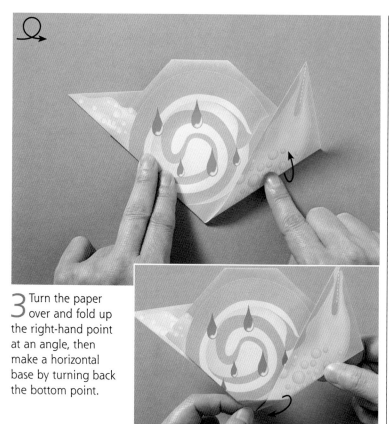

3 Turn the paper over and fold up the right-hand point at an angle, then make a horizontal base by turning back the bottom point.

4 Turn the model over again and use the scissors to cut between the antennae on the design, following the dotted line. To finish, give them shape by curling them around a pencil.

19 **HATO** PIGEON

It is believed that pigeons have been reared for use as homing birds for well over 6,000 years. They are now common in every city of the world, as well as being used for transferring messages and racing across long distances. This model is quick to make as well as being extremely simple—after forming the first diamond shape, just three more folds are required.

You will need:
1 sheet of 6 in (15 cm) square paper

1 With the design side facing down, fold the paper in half from corner to corner through the design and open out. Fold the left-hand edges over so that they meet along the central crease, then turn the right-hand edges over in the same way.

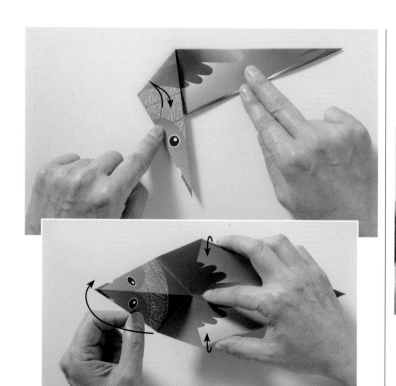

2 Fold the model in half along the central crease.

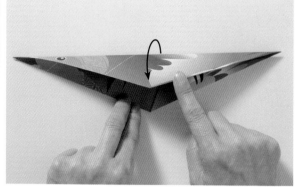

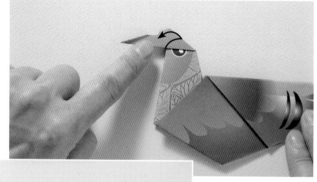

3 Fold the left-hand end over at an angle, using the dotted line on the design as a guide, then lift the paper off the table and open it. Turn the left-hand point up using the creases just made and press the two sides together around it.

4 Fold the left-hand tip forward at an angle to make a crease, then open up the flap and refold it inside, reversing the direction of the creases where necessary.

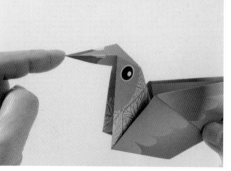

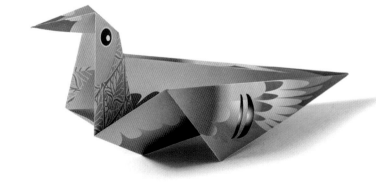

20 **KUJYAKU** PEACOCK

This colorful bird is the male peacock, showing off the long, bright feathers of its tail which it can lift and fan out when it is particularly pleased with itself. Even when at rest with its tail down, it is a spectacular sight which is recreated in this *origami* model.

You will need:
1 sheet of 6 in (15 cm) square paper

IN THE GARDEN

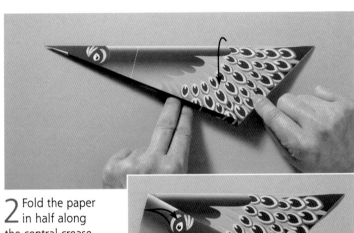

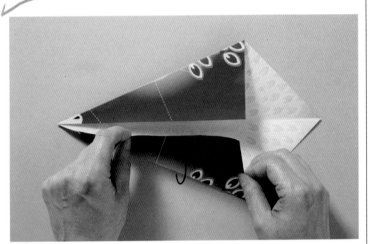

1 With the design side facing down, fold the paper in half from corner to corner through the design and open out. Fold the left-hand edges over so that they meet along the central crease.

2 Fold the paper in half along the central crease, then fold back the left-hand point at an angle, using the dotted line on the design as a guide, to make a crease.

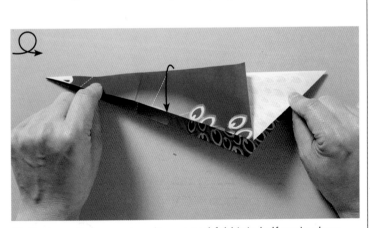

3 Open up the paper, turn it over, and fold it in half again along the central crease.

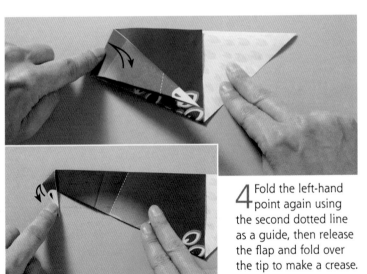

4 Fold the left-hand point again using the second dotted line as a guide, then release the flap and fold over the tip to make a crease.

5 Turn the paper over and open it up, then carefully form a concertina fold using the two central creases. As you form the neck of the bird close the body around it. Finish by refolding the tip inside to make the beak, using the second crease made in the previous step.

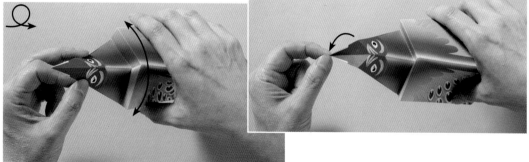

PART THREE
ON THE FARM

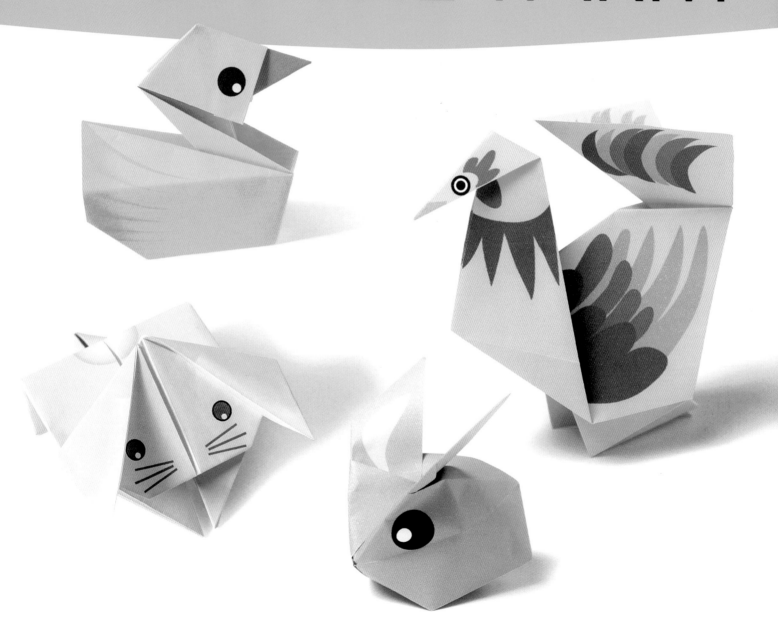

21 BUTA PIG

Although somethimes thought of as a bit dirty, pigs are actually very good at keeping themselves clean—just like this pristine *origami* model. If you are unhappy with the way the two sides of the back look as if they are coming apart after you have finished, you can stick them together with paper glue.

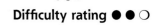
You will need:
1 sheet of 6 in (15 cm) square paper

1 With the design side facing down fold the paper in half from side to side both ways, opening out each time, then fold the bottom and top edges in to meet along the central crease.

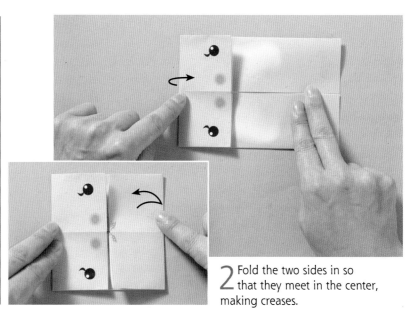

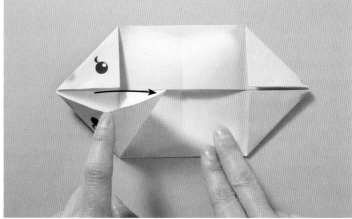

2 Fold the two sides in so that they meet in the center, making creases.

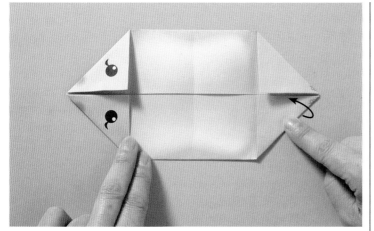

3 Open out the folds and turn the corners over at 45° so that the paper's edges align along the center line.

4 Open out each flap and pull out the corner of paper, turning it along the center line and folding it flat to create a triangular flap.

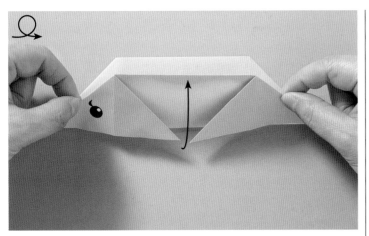

5 Turn the paper over and fold the model in half along the central crease.

6 Turn the inner half of each triangular flap toward the outside of the model so that the diagonal edge now runs vertically.

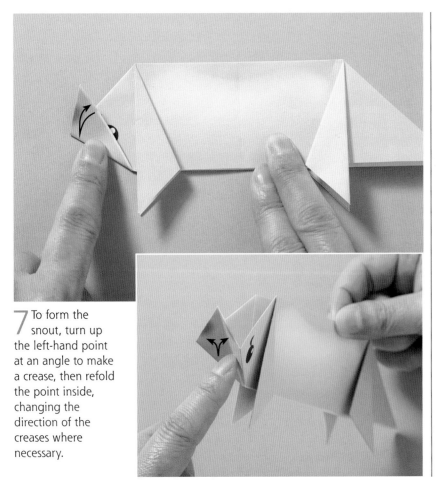

7 To form the snout, turn up the left-hand point at an angle to make a crease, then refold the point inside, changing the direction of the creases where necessary.

8 Turn over the very tip of the snout in the same way and fold this inside as well to give it a flat top.

9 Fold up the model's right-hand point at an angle so that the bottom edge runs vertically, making a crease, then open the end out again and make a second angled crease between the paper's bottom edge and the crease just made.

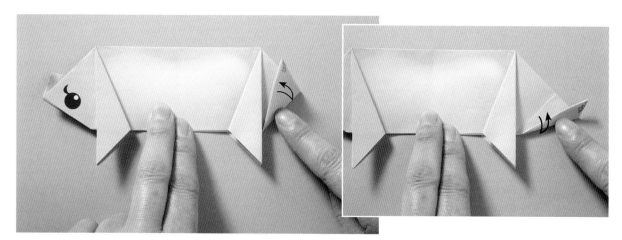

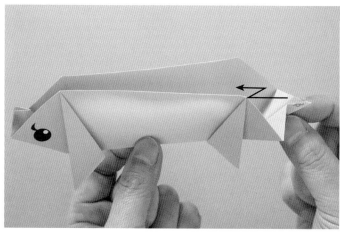

10 Fold the right-hand end inside the body of the model using the two creases just made to form a concertina fold. Take care to change the direction of some of the creases to make this work. Next, fold the new right-hand points inside to give the rear of the model a straight edge.

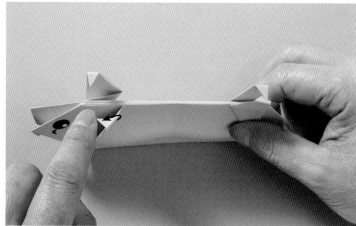

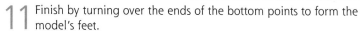

11 Finish by turning over the ends of the bottom points to form the model's feet.

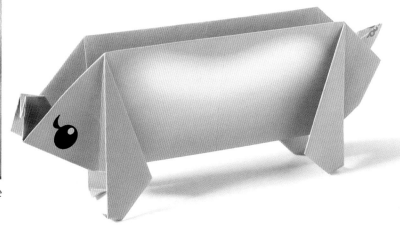

22 **USAGI** RABBIT

Rabbits playing hide-and-seek in the farmyard are so cute. They come out of their burrows when all is quiet but hide again as soon as anyone appears. This *origami* model is very similar to the traditional Japanese balloon and also needs to be inflated by blowing in air through a straw. The last step is a little difficult so check no air escapes.

Difficulty rating ● ● ●

You will need:
1 sheet of 6 in (15 cm) square paper
Drinking straw

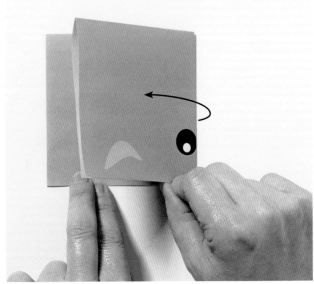

1 Fold the paper in half through the design, then fold in half again.

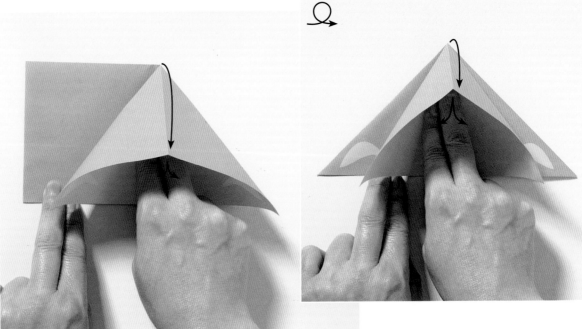

2 Lift the flap, open it out, and refold it into a triangle. Turn the paper over and repeat on the other side.

3 Fold the upper flaps of each side point up to the top point so that the bottom edges align with each other along the central crease.

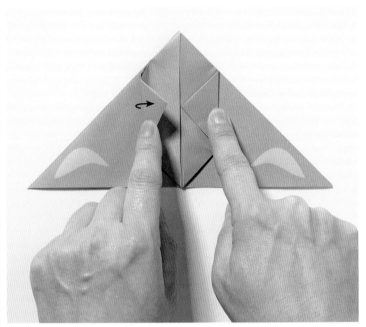

4 Fold the new side points of the same flaps in so that they meet in the middle of the model.

5 Turn over the top points of the same flaps so that the edges align with the folds made in the previous step.

6 Turn the flap made in the previous step over the diagonal edge to make a crease and release. Now lift the side flaps and carefully open up the pocket so that you can feed in the flap just made.

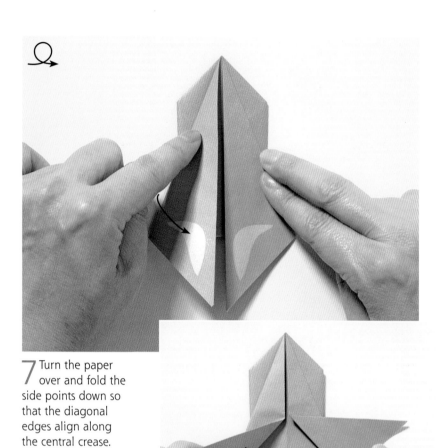

7 Turn the paper over and fold the side points down so that the diagonal edges align along the central crease. Next, turn the bottom points out to the sides, ensuring that the top edges are horizontal.

8 Fold both sides up so that the horizontal bottom edges of the model now align up the central crease.

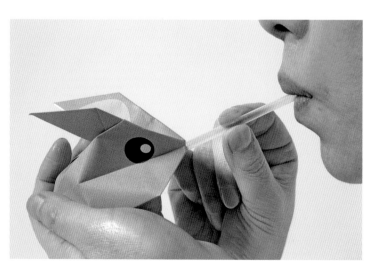

9 Gently lift the paper off the table and begin to prise it open. Next, use the drinking straw to blow air inside the model through the hole in its nose until it is completely inflated.

23 TAREMIMI USAGI
HOPPING RABBIT

When you have made this *origami* model of a Holland Lop, a special breed of rabbit famous for leaping high in the air when it feels happy, you can make it jump up and down as well. Although it starts in a similar way to the *origami* frog (see page 52) the second half is a little trickier as you have many intricate folds to make.

You will need:

1 sheet of 6 in (15 cm) square paper

1 Fold the paper from side to side both ways, opening out each time to make creases, then fold the left-hand end in so the edge runs along the central crease.

2 Fold the two left-hand corners over at an angle so that they meet on the center line, then open the flaps, pull out the corner of paper from inside, and turn it along the center line, flattening it to make a new triangular flap.

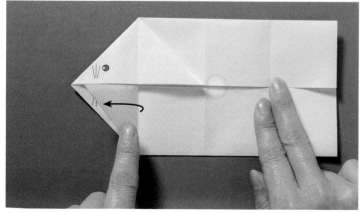

3 Fold the two loose points of the new triangular folds back over to the left-hand end of the model.

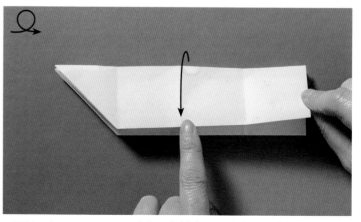

4 Turn the paper over and then fold the model in half along the central crease.

79

TAREMIMI USAGI HOPPING RABBIT

5 Fold over the upper flap at the left-hand end, then lift the newly revealed flap to the vertical and push the point forward and down, refolding it into a diamond shape. Fold the bottom tip of the diamond underneath itself to give the newly formed face a flat bottom edge.

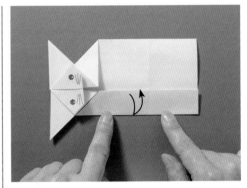

6 Open up the model and find the horizontal creases underneath the face. Press the outer ends of these creases together and flat so that the creases run together down the model's central crease.

7 Fold the long edges over to the center of the model to make creases.

8 Open out these last folds and fold the right-hand end of the model over to the existing edges underneath the head, then fold the newly made flap over on itself.

9 Lift the short top edge to the vertical and pull the loose corner of paper over to the right, refolding it flat while ensuring it has a diagonal, creased edge. Repeat on the bottom.

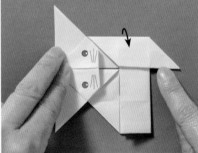

10 Open the top flap by lifting the edge up to the vertical and also gently lift up the top side of the head. Find the middle of the horizontal edge of paper and turn it up and across to the center line, underneath the face, then fold the flap back down. Repeat on the bottom.

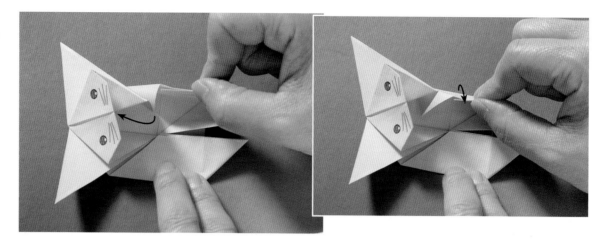

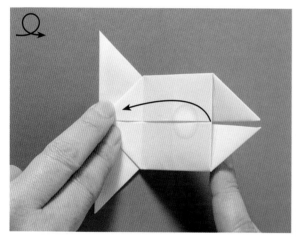

11 Turn the paper over and fold the right-hand point over to the left.

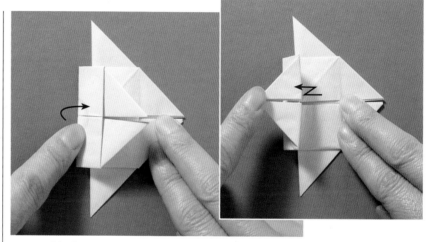

12 Fold what are now the left-hand points back so that they sit on the vertical crease, then fold the points back on themselves again over the vertical edges.

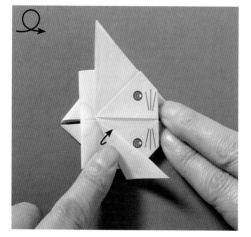

13 Turn the model over and fold the remaining tips over at an angle to make the ears, ensuring that the edges do not cover the eyes.

24 **AHIRU** DUCK

You can make two pretty ducks from the one piece of paper supplied, each one swimming happily across the farmyard pond. Although usually brightly colored, you could use plain paper to make more—just remember to draw on and color the eyes and beak when you have finished folding the model into shape.

You will need:
1 sheet of 6 in (15 cm) square paper
Scissors

1 Cut the sheet of paper in half with the scissors and use one side to make each duck.

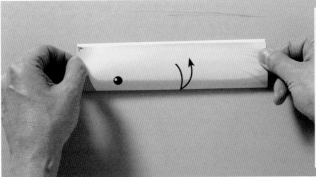 

2 Fold the paper in half to make a crease, then open it out and fold the two long edges in to meet along the central crease.

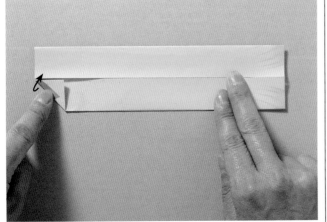

3 Fold the left-hand corners over so that they meet along the center line.

4 Fold over the left-hand end, using the dotted lines on the design as a guide, then fold back the tip in a concertina fold.

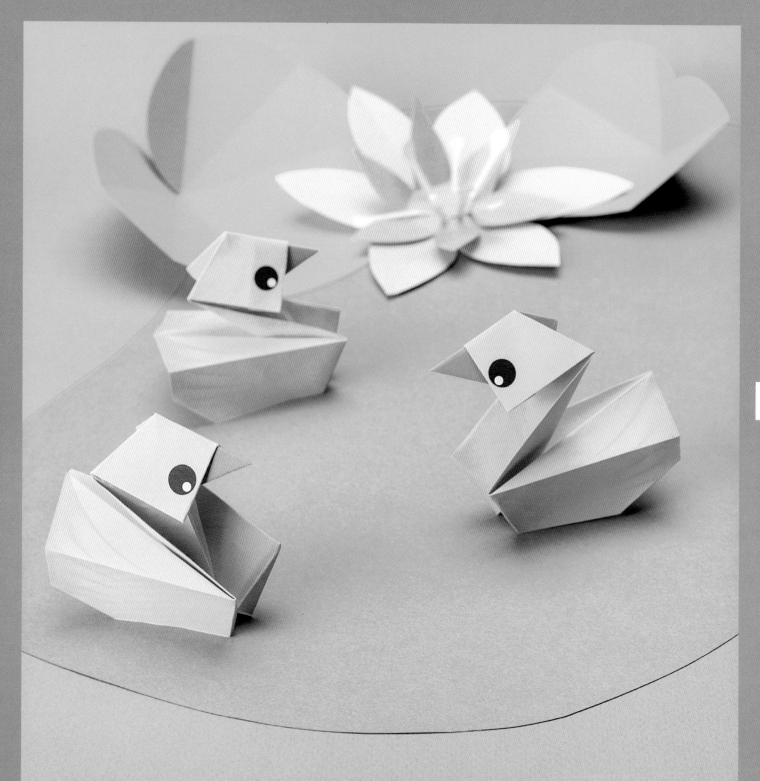

5 Turn over the left-hand end at an angle and make a crease from the bottom edge to the center line, then repeat on the other side.

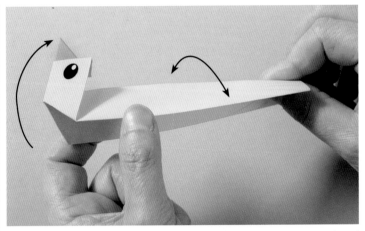

6 Lift the paper and press the long sides together, allowing the head to become an outside fold surrounding the main length of paper.

7 With the model back on the table, open up the body and press the top edge of paper along the base of the head, making a diagonal crease across to the central crease. Repeat on the other side, then use these creases to make another outside fold to surround the head.

8 Fold the length of paper in half to make a crease, using the dotted line given on the design as a guide.

9 Carefully open out the body and then turn it back on itself using the crease made in the last step.

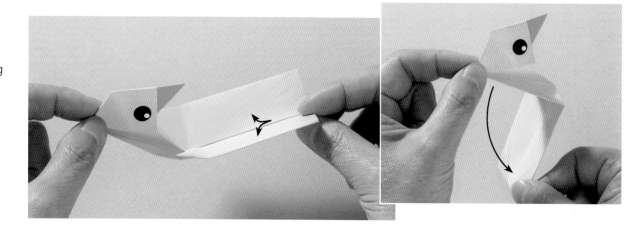

10 Check that you end up with the body around the neck and parallel to the head.

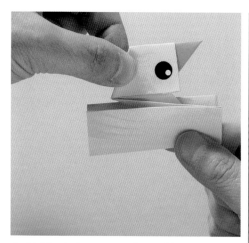

11 Holding the model on the table, gently pull down the left-hand end of the upper flap and press down to form a new diagonal crease. Turn the model over and repeat on the other side.

12 Fold the bottom corners at the rear of the model to the inside.

25 ITACHI FERRET

A ferret is a popular type of pet weasel which is sometimes used to catch rabbits, though it is famous for its very sharp teeth and may bite you if you are not careful. It is probably much safer to play with this pretty *origami* model than the real thing, so don't give up if at first you find some of the design tricky to follow.

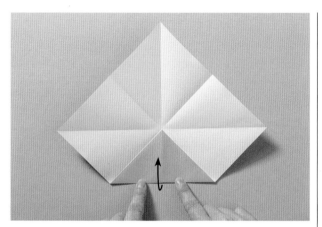

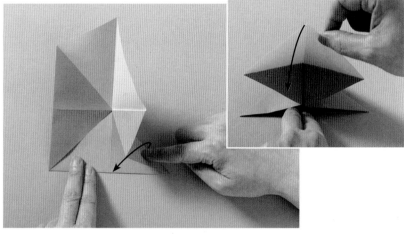

1 Take the sheet of paper with the design for the head and place it with the design side facing down on the table. Fold it in half from side to side both ways, opening out each time, then both ways from corner to corner. Next, fold in the bottom point and two side points so that they meet in the center.

2 Fold the middle of each side over and down so that they meet in the middle of the bottom edge, then fold the top point over to the bottom, to create a large diamond shape.

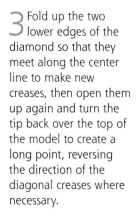

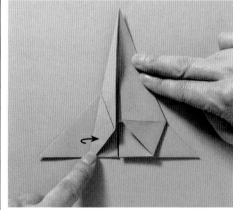

3 Fold up the two lower edges of the diamond so that they meet along the center line to make new creases, then open them up again and turn the tip back over the top of the model to create a long point, reversing the direction of the diagonal creases where necessary.

4 Fold in the two diagonal edges so that they meet along the center line.

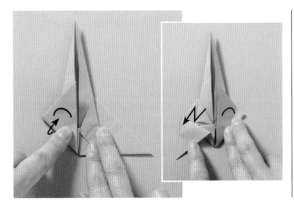

5 Fold up the two outer points so that the two halves of the bottom edge align along the center line and then turn the points back down to form concertina folds.

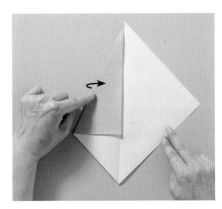

6 Take the second sheet and, design side facing down, fold it in half from corner to corner through the design to make a crease, then open it up again and fold the two upper edges in so that they align along the central crease.

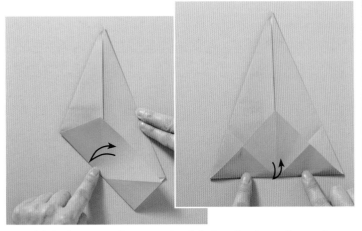

7 Fold the bottom point up to the right-hand point and press flat to make a crease, then open out and repeat on the other side. Open out again and fold the bottom point up between the outer points to make a third crease.

8 Fold the outer points across to meet on the center line, then fold up the remaining point to sit on top of them and form a diamond-shaped flap.

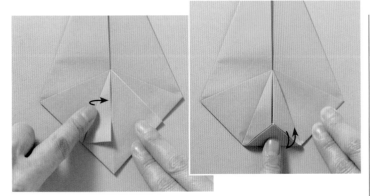

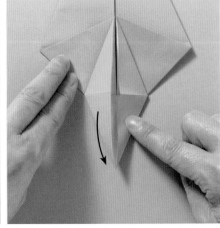

9 Fold in the upper edges of this diamond so that they meet along the central crease, then turn up the bottom point to make a crease across the bottom of the two flaps just made.

10 Open up the flaps made in the last step and turn the top point of the diamond down to form a long diamond, reversing the direction of the edge creases where necessary.

ON THE FARM

12 Carefully slip the bottom corners of the flaps made in the last step underneath the edge of the diamond made earlier.

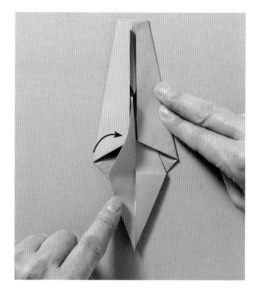

11 Fold down the top point so that it touches the flaps made across the bottom of the model, then fold in the upper edges so that they meet along the center line.

13 Now form the shape of the ferret's body by holding the right-hand end of the model down on the table while gently pulling up the left-hand point to the vertical. Next, carefully press the two sides of the pointed end together and re-form the creases at the base of this point so that it retains its new shape.

14 Pick up the head again and fit it into the space inside the top of the body.

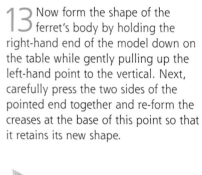

ITACHI FERRET

26 NIWATORI CHICKEN

No farmyard would be complete without a chicken striding purposefully across it looking for grain or seeds to peck at. This is a tricky model to make so follow the instructions closely and always check that the pattern you see on your own model matches that shown in the photograph. Remember that the more precise your folds at the beginning, the easier the later steps will be.

You will need:
1 sheet of 6 in (15 cm) square paper
Scissors

1 Fold the paper in half through the design to make a crease and open out. Fold in the right-hand edges so that they meet along the central crease.

2 Turn the paper over and fold the left-hand end, making a crease between the top and bottom points. Turn the paper back over and fold up the top and bottom points so that the edges align along the central crease.

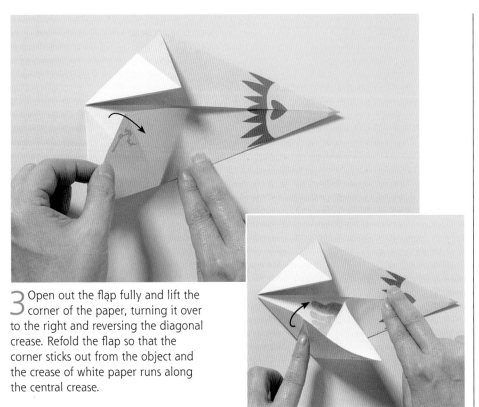

3 Open out the flap fully and lift the corner of the paper, turning it over to the right and reversing the diagonal crease. Refold the flap so that the corner sticks out from the object and the crease of white paper runs along the central crease.

4 Turn back the points that are sticking out so that their edge runs down the diagonal edge of white paper.

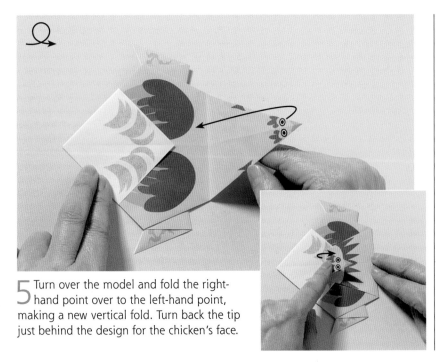

5 Turn over the model and fold the right-hand point over to the left-hand point, making a new vertical fold. Turn back the tip just behind the design for the chicken's face.

6 Pick up the model and fold it in half along the central crease.

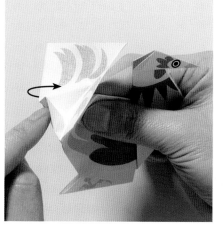

7 Holding the main body of the chicken, pull the neck forward and make new creases. Now lift the head away from the neck in the same way and make new creases. Press flat.

8 Turn over the top point on the left at an angle, then open out the model and refold the tip inside, reversing the direction of the creases.

9 Take the pair of scissors and carefully cut up both of the folds of white paper at the back end of the model, then gently reverse the folds so that the design is visible.

10 Carefully open up the tail and fold the end point inside to form the structure of the tail.

27 UMA HORSE

This *origami* horse is a delightful model and, when running about in its paddock, it gives a true feeling of freedom. Make the body first, taking care when expanding the paper in the middle. Folding the head can be hard because of the many sheets of paper that lie on top of each other, but do your best.

Difficulty rating: ● ● ●

You will need:
2 sheets of 6 in (15 cm) square paper
Paper glue

1 Fold the sheet that makes the horse's body in half both ways to make creases, opening it out each time. Turn in the sides so that they meet along the central crease, then turn in both ends so that they also meet.

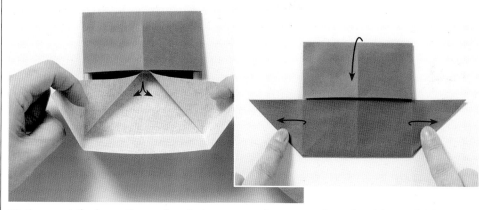

2 Open out the lower flap and push the corners of paper out from the object, refolding them so that they form triangular flaps on either side. Repeat at the top.

3 Turn the object over and fold the top and bottom edges over so that they meet along the central crease of the object.

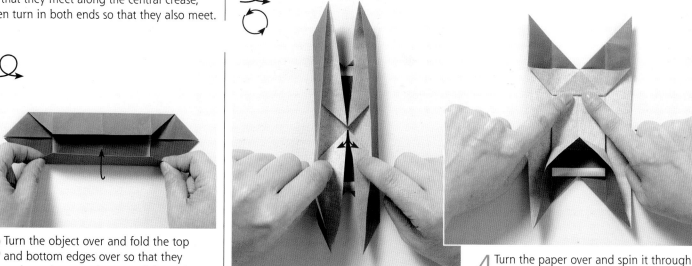

4 Turn the paper over and spin it through 90°, then gently open out the model, folding the edges over so that they lie flat.

5 Fold the object in half across itself to form the basic shape of the horse's body. Make new folds on the insides of every leg, creating crease lines from the ends of the legs to the middle of the top edge of the model.

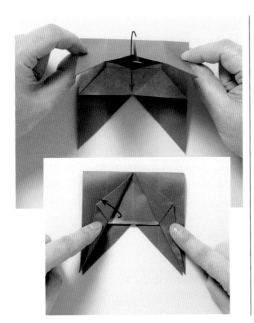

6 Fold over the top left corner of the object, then open up the model and refold the corner inside, reversing the direction of the creases. Put the body aside till later.

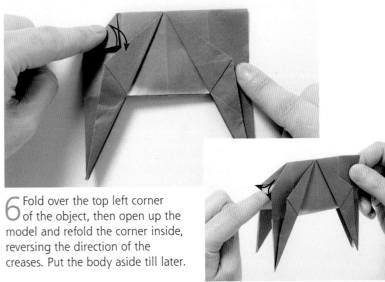

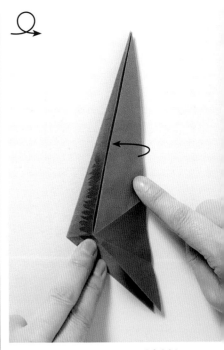

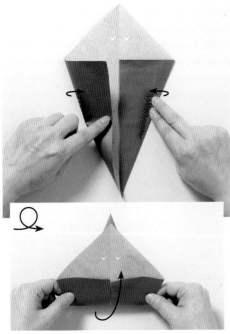

7 Fold the second sheet in half from corner to corner through the design to make a crease, then open it out and fold the lower edges in so that they meet along this central crease. Turn the paper over and fold the object in half.

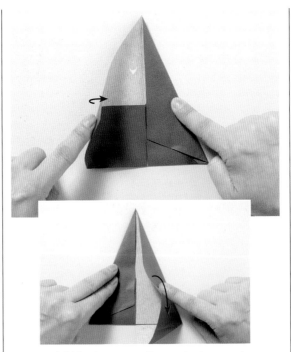

8 Next fold in the upper diagonal edges so that they meet along the central crease. Carefully open up these new flaps and pull out the corner of paper from inside, refolding it below the base of the model, to form a diamond shape.

9 Turn the paper over and fold it in half lengthwise.

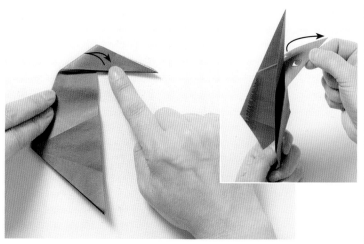

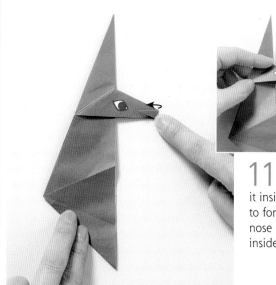

10 Fold over the pointed tip at right angles to the main body of the model to make a crease. Release the end, then lift the paper up and carefully pull forward the outer layer of the creased end, reversing the direction of the folds to make an outside fold.

11 Turn back the tip, then refold it inside the head to form the horse's nose using an inside fold.

12 Fold down the remaining part of the top point, making a crease inside the neck below the level of the head. Carefully open up the back of the neck and refold it, this time reversing the creases using an inside fold.

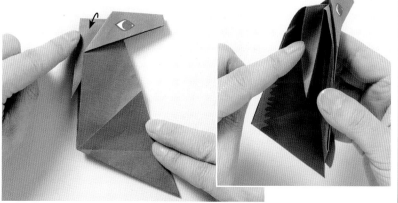

13 Fold forward the back of the neck on both sides to reveal the design of the horse's mane.

14 Using a little bit of paper glue, join the two parts together, sliding the neck around the body inside the flaps of the legs.

PART FOUR
IN THE WILD

28 SEKISEI INKO PARAKEET

Parakeets are not only charming birds that can be friendly companions as they chirrup and chatter in the house, but have also become common in almost every large city in the world, swooping between the trees in parks. Now you can make your own so that the flash of green plumage is always visible.

You will need:
1 sheet of 6 in (15 cm) square paper
Scissors

1 With the design side facing down, fold the paper in half from corner to corner both ways, opening up each time, and then from side to side. Then fold the corners in to meet at the center. Fold the two corners made on the left-hand side into the center.

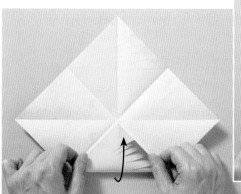

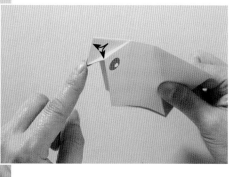

2 Fold the paper in half along the central crease, then turn down the left-hand tip at an angle to make a crease. Refold the tip inside, reversing the direction of the creases where necessary.

3 Using the scissors, cut up the diagonal crease from the bottom right corner to a point opposite the base of the eye.

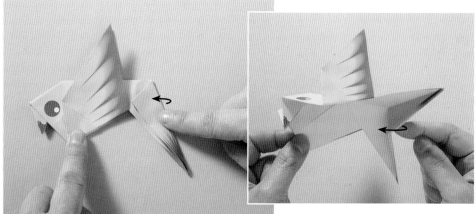

4 Fold up the bottom edge at an angle between the top of the cut and the left-hand edge, ensuring that the flap does not cover the eye. Turn over and repeat on the other side.

5 Fold the right-hand edge over at an angle so that it runs up the diagonal edge, then open up the model and refold inside, reversing the direction of the creases where necessary.

29 OUMU PARROT

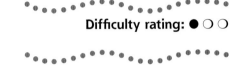
The beautifully colored parrot is not only a common sight in the jungles of the world but is also famous for sitting on a pirate's shoulder, repeating the words he has learnt from his master. This *origami* model is extremely easy to make in just a few simple steps—but take care to fold the beak at a realistic angle.

You will need:
1 sheet of 6 in (15 cm) square paper

102

IN THE WILD

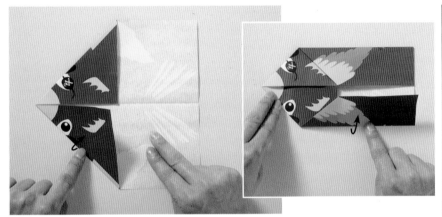

1 With the design side facing down, fold the paper in half through the design to make a crease and open out, then fold the left-hand points over to meet at the center. Next, fold in the top and bottom edges to meet along the central crease.

2 Turn the paper over and fold it in half along the central crease.

3 Fold down the right-hand end at right angles to form a diagonal crease, starting just to the right of the existing crease, then open up the model and refold the end inside, reversing the direction of the creases where necessary.

4 Fold the bottom left-hand corner of the new flap up and across along the horizonal edge to form a new crease, then open up the model and refold it inside, reversing the direction of the creases where necessary.

5 Fold over the left-hand point of the model at an angle to form a crease, then open up the model and refold the point inside to form the parrot's beak.

30 NIHON ZARU MONKEY

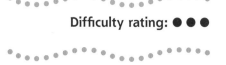

As well as living in the forests and hills the Japanese macaque is famous for enjoying the warm water of hot springs in winter—what better way of keeping out the cold than a nice, hot bath? Start the model with a kite fold, then use the dotted lines on the design to ensure the monkey ends up in the correct shape.

You will need:
1 sheet of 6 in (15 cm) square paper

1 With the design side facing down, fold the paper in half through the design to make a crease and open out, then fold in the top and right-hand edges so that they meet along the central crease.

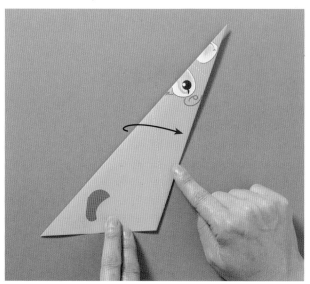

2 Fold the paper in half along the central crease.

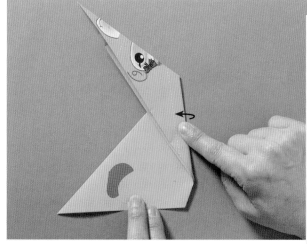

3 Turn over the top point to the left with a slightly angled crease, then turn the tip back to the right so that it is parallel to the first crease to make a concertina fold.

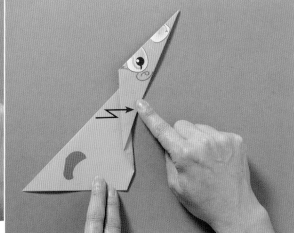

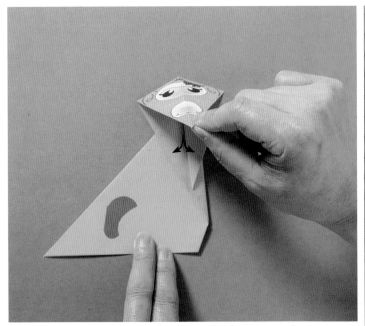

4 Lift the top point back up to the vertical, then fold it forward, pressing the paper flat to form the face.

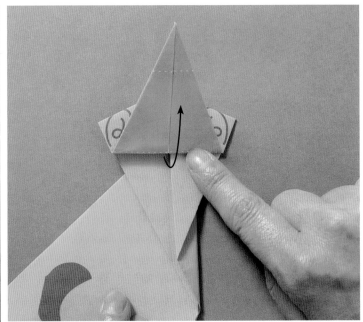

5 Fold up the bottom point of the face to make a crease, using the dotted line printed on the design as a guide.

IN THE WILD

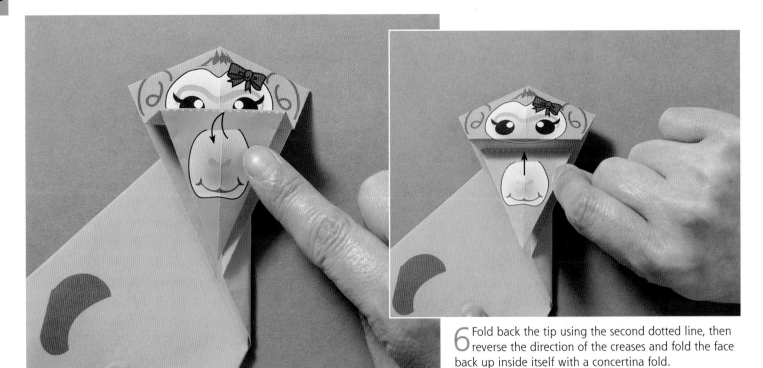

6 Fold back the tip using the second dotted line, then reverse the direction of the creases and fold the face back up inside itself with a concertina fold.

7 Fold the tip of the nose back underneath itself to create a flat nose for your monkey.

8 Turn over the left-hand end at an angle to make a crease, then open up the model and refold the tip inside, reversing the direction of the creases where necessary.

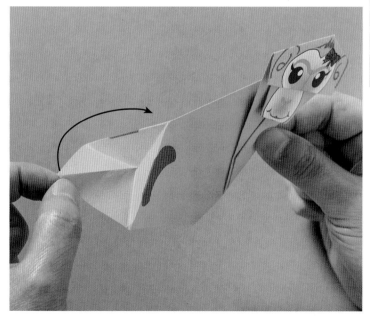

9 Fold up the inside crease at an angle and press it flat to form the tail, ensuring that the base of the model is completely flat.

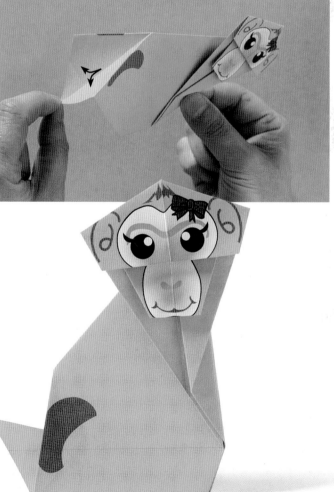

31 HEBI SNAKE

The snake's long body slips and slides across the ground as it moves through the grass, the repeated pattern on its body camouflaging it so that its prey cannot see it approach. If you take care to make the first fold completely even, the pattern will repeat perfectly.

You will need:
1 sheet of 6 in (15 cm) square paper

108

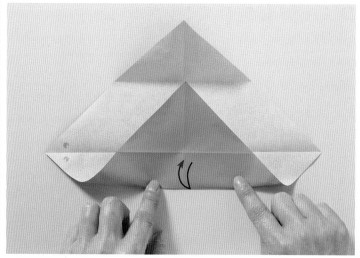

1 With the design side facing down, fold the paper in half from corner to corner both ways, opening out each time, then fold in the top and bottom points so that they meet at the crossing of the creases.

2 Open out the paper and fold the bottom edge up to the top crease. Make a new crease, then open up the paper and repeat, folding the top point to the lowest crease.

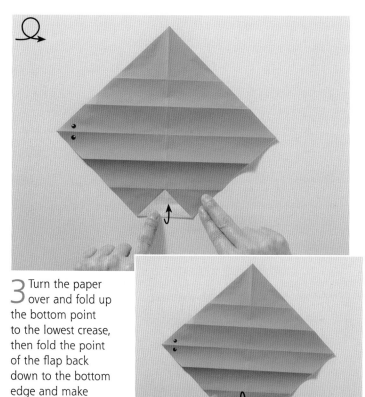

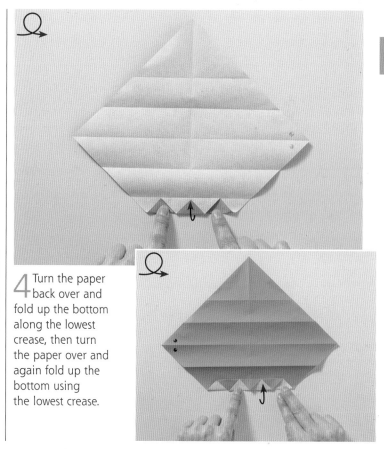

3 Turn the paper over and fold up the bottom point to the lowest crease, then fold the point of the flap back down to the bottom edge and make another crease.

4 Turn the paper back over and fold up the bottom along the lowest crease, then turn the paper over and again fold up the bottom using the lowest crease.

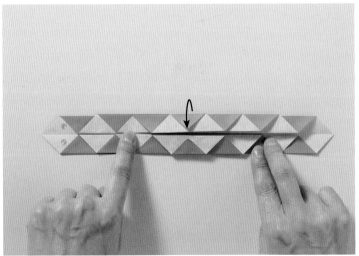

5 Continue turning the paper over and folding up, using the lowest crease each time, until you reach the central crease.

6 Repeat the process from the top until both sides meet along the central crease.

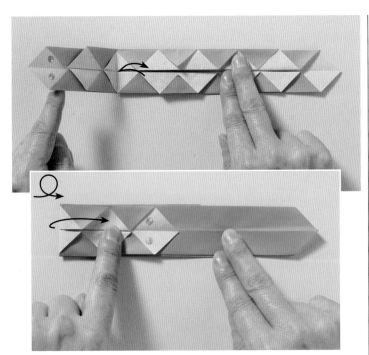

7 Turn the left-hand end over to the right, making a crease through the center of the third white diamond, then turn the paper over and reverse the direction of the crease.

8 Carefully turn over the left-hand corners at angles to make creases.

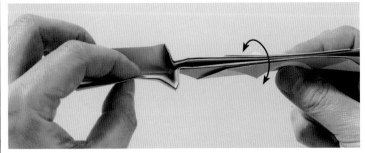

9 Lift the paper off the table and open the model out to its full length, releasing the flaps made in the last step, then press the sides together.

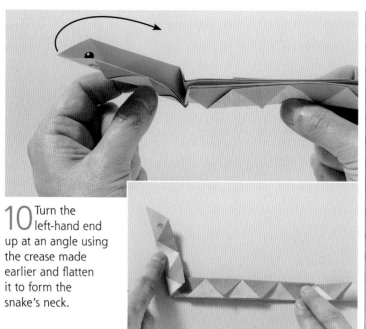

10 Turn the left-hand end up at an angle using the crease made earlier and flatten it to form the snake's neck.

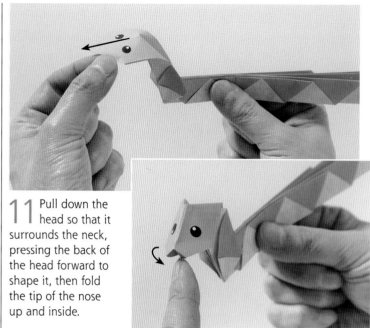

11 Pull down the head so that it surrounds the neck, pressing the back of the head forward to shape it, then fold the tip of the nose up and inside.

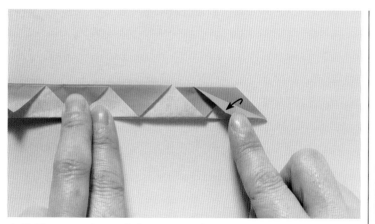

12 Turn over the angled corners at the right-hand end so that the diagonal edges now run along the bottom edge.

13 Finish by inserting creases into the body of the snake to make it stand up and look like it is moving.

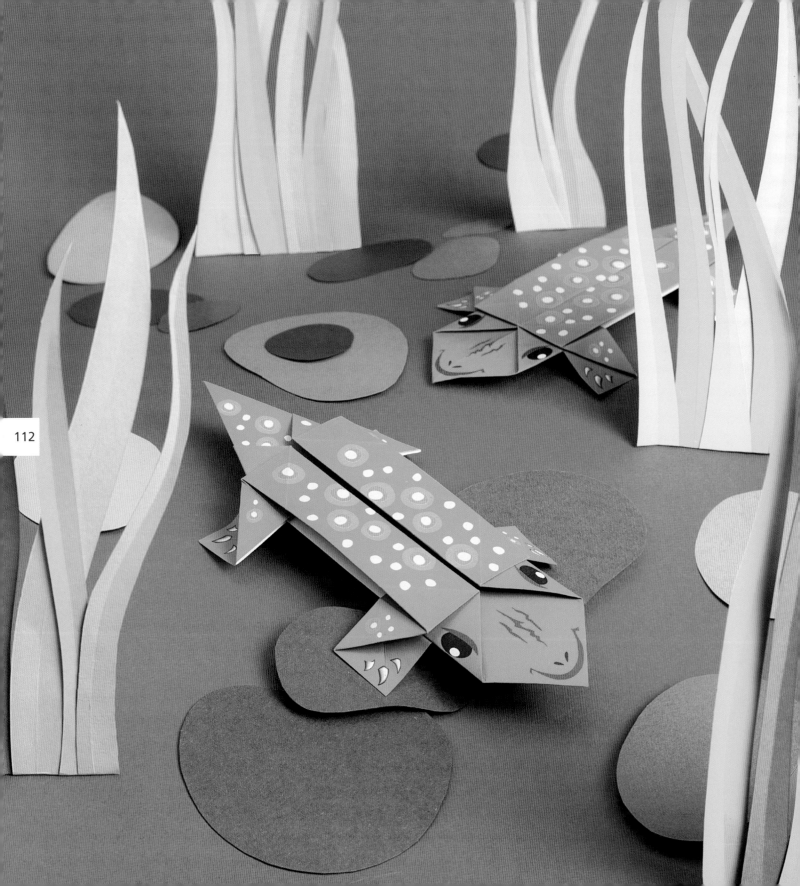

32 TOKAGE LIZARD

Lizards are easiest to see in the wild early in the morning, basking in the sunlight as the day warms up and rousing themselves after a cold night. Later they are a fascinating sight as they dart between hiding places. Nowadays they are also a common pet, though it can be a bit surprising to see how large they can grow.

Difficulty rating: ● ● ●

You will need:
1 sheet of 6 in (15 cm) square paper

1 With the design side facing down, fold the paper in half from corner to corner both ways, opening out each time, then fold in the corners so that they meet at the crossing of the creases.

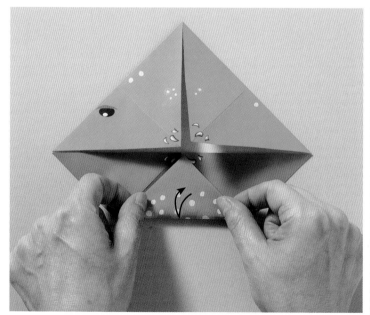

2 Next fold in the top and bottom points so that they meet in the center of the paper, making horizontal creases.

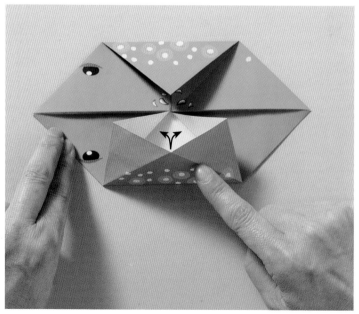

3 Open up the bottom flap and gently pull apart the centers of the two adjoining edges of paper and then fold down the newly created bottom edge along the center line of the model. Repeat on the top flap.

4 Turn the paper over and fold the top and bottom edges over so that they meet in the center of the model.

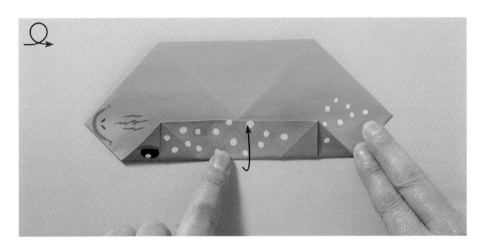

5 Turn the paper back over and open the flap from the middle downward. As the sides of the flap lift, press each corner of paper down and across onto the relevant corner of the new bottom edge. Again, repeat at the top.

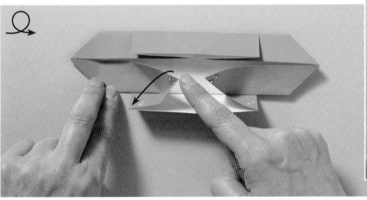

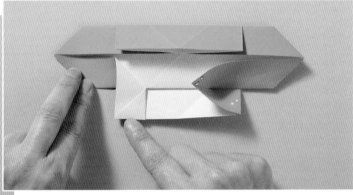

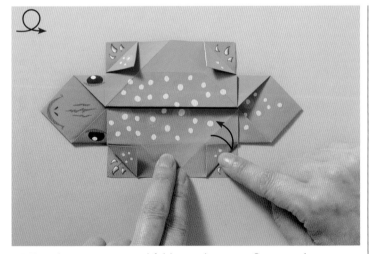

6 Turn the paper over and fold over the upper flap at each corner to form new diagonal creases across the corners.

7 Lift the bottom edge, releasing the flaps made in the last step.

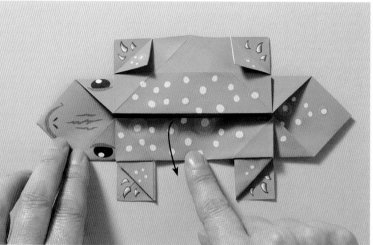

8 Carefully fold the edge back underneath itself using the existing horizontal crease. Let the corners fold in on themselves using the creases made in Step 6.

9 To finish, turn the paper over and fold in the diagonal edges at the right-hand end so that they meet along the center line.

33 YADOKARI HERMIT CRAB

The hermit crab does not grow a shell of its own; instead it searches for an empty shell to climb inside which will protect it from dangerous predators. As the crab grows and gets larger its home becomes a tighter squeeze with less and less space, so it has to discard the shell and find a new one to live in.

You will need:
1 sheet of 6 in (15 cm) square paper

1 With the design side facing down, fold the paper in half from corner to corner both ways.

IN THE WILD

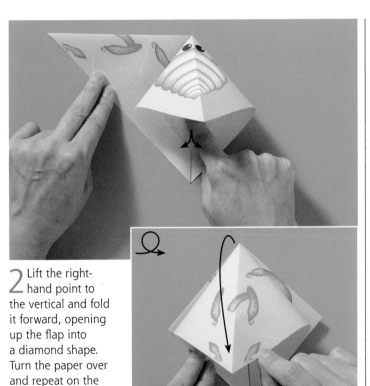

2 Lift the right-hand point to the vertical and fold it forward, opening up the flap into a diamond shape. Turn the paper over and repeat on the other side.

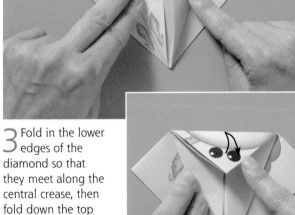

3 Fold in the lower edges of the diamond so that they meet along the central crease, then fold down the top point over the edges of these flaps to make a crease.

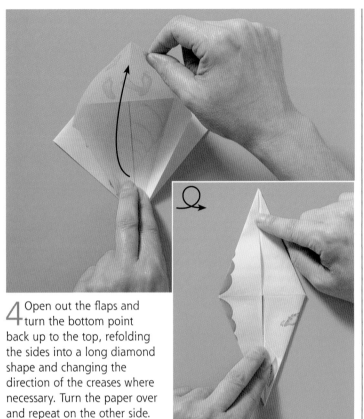

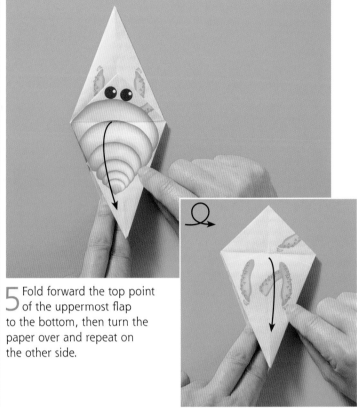

4 Open out the flaps and turn the bottom point back up to the top, refolding the sides into a long diamond shape and changing the direction of the creases where necessary. Turn the paper over and repeat on the other side.

5 Fold forward the top point of the uppermost flap to the bottom, then turn the paper over and repeat on the other side.

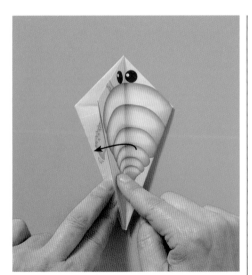

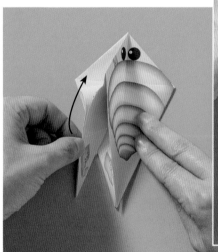

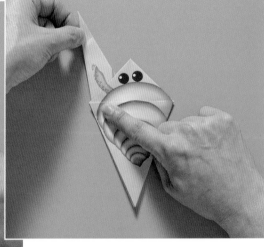

6 Turn the uppermost point on the right-hand side over to the left.

7 Carefully reopen the flap just made and pull out the uppermost point of paper from inside. As it is turned upward it will reverse the direction in which it is folded. Find the point where the two parts of the design meet and press it down.

8 Pull out the second point from inside the left-hand flap and turn it up in the same way, folding it right up to the vertical. Press down flat.

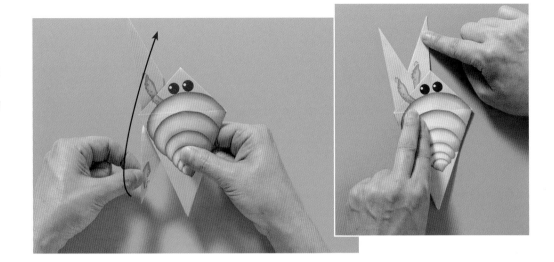

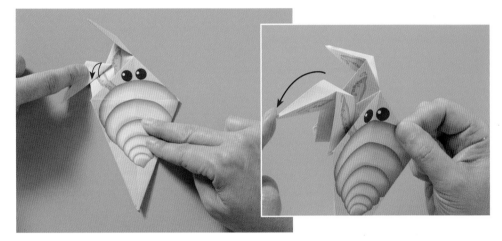

9 Fold over the points of both these flaps to the left at an angle, then open up each flap and refold the tips inside.

10 Finish by folding up the bottom point of the model at an angle to make a crease, then fold both parts of the bottom point inside the model.

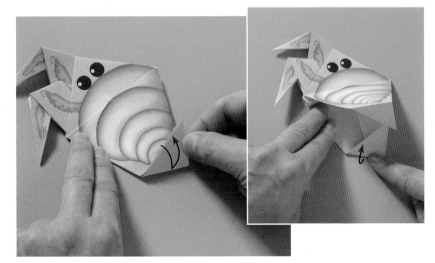

34 **NETAIGYO** ANGEL FISH

Difficulty rating: ● ● ●

You will need:
1 sheet of 6 in (15 cm) square paper

The colorful angel fish swims around the reefs and islands of the world's hot seas and is easy to spot if you go swimming with a mask. This *origami* model is based on the method of making the crane, one of the most traditional *origami* designs. As you finish, let the body open up to give it a three-dimensional feeling.

1 With the design side facing down, fold the paper in half from corner to corner both ways.

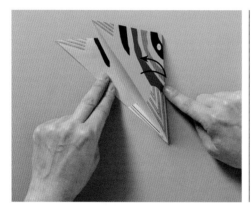

2 Lift the right-hand point to the vertical and fold it forward, opening up the flap into a diamond shape. Turn the paper over and repeat on the other side.

3 Fold in the lower edges of the diamond so that they meet along the central crease, then fold down the top point over the edges of these flaps to make a crease.

4 Open out the flaps and turn the bottom point back up to the top, refolding the sides into a long diamond shape.

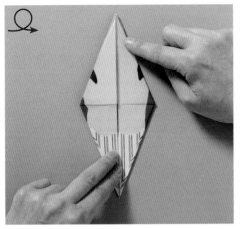

5 Turn the paper over and repeat on the other side.

6 Fold forward the top point of the uppermost flap to the bottom and then turn the paper over and repeat on the other side.

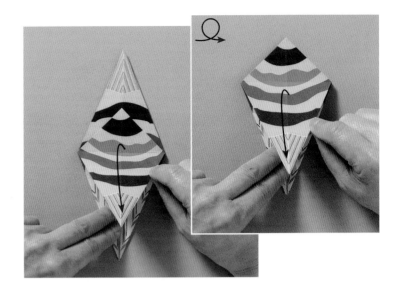

7 Fold the bottom point of the uppermost flap over so that the point sits on the model's top point.

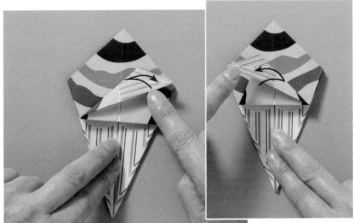

8 Fold the same point over to the right-hand corner of the model and make a diagonal crease, then do the same thing to the left.

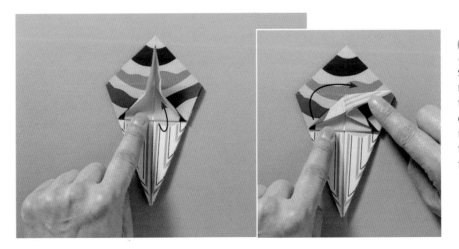

9 Lift the point up and press the sides of the flap nearest the point together, using the diagonal creases just made, then press the whole flap over, flat to the right.

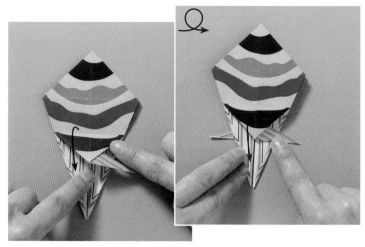

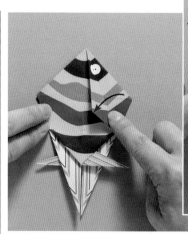

10 Fold the same flap down over the central horizontal crease line, then turn the model over and repeat the whole process on the other side.

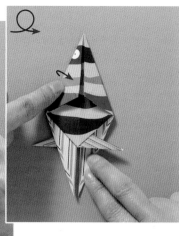

11 Fold in the upper diagonal edges so that they meet along the central vertical crease. Turn over and repeat.

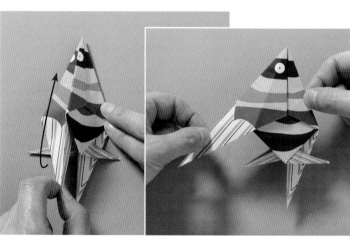

12 Let the left-hand side of the model open and pull out the long point from inside, turning it round to the top. The direction in which the flap is folded will reverse and the creases made in the last step will open up. Repeat on the other side of the fish.

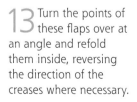

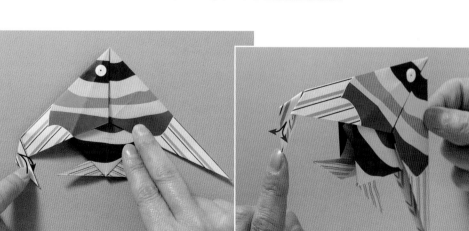

13 Turn the points of these flaps over at an angle and refold them inside, reversing the direction of the creases where necessary.

35 **FUGU** BLOWFISH

The gently swelling blowfish—one of Japan's greatest delicacies—is famous for its taste but remember to be careful, as the wrong parts are very poisonous if eaten! You might notice that this model closely resembles the traditional *origami* balloon—both need to be blown up to make their shape—but you can also use your finger to give it the ideal shape.

You will need:
1 sheet of 6 in (15 cm) square paper

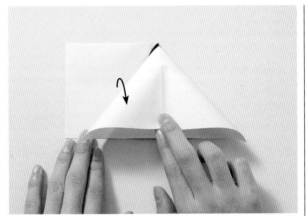

1 Fold the paper in half between the eyes and in half again, making a crease, then lift the top flap and make a triangle fold.

2 Fold up the outer points of the upper flaps so that they meet at the top point, forming a diamond, then fold in the outer points of the diamond to meet on the center line.

3 Fold down the two loose tips at the top of the object so that their edges run along the edges made in the previous step. Tuck these doubled-over flaps into the pockets on the diagonal edges and flatten.

4 Turn the model over and fold each side in half so that their diagonal edges align along the center line, then fold the bottom left-hand tip back out to the sides, making a crease from the outer corner to the center line.

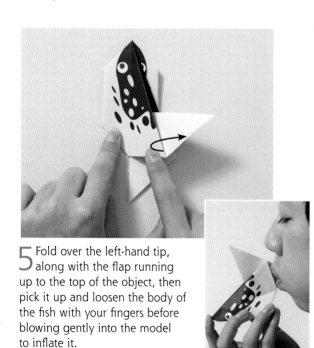

5 Fold over the left-hand tip, along with the flap running up to the top of the object, then pick it up and loosen the body of the fish with your fingers before blowing gently into the model to inflate it.

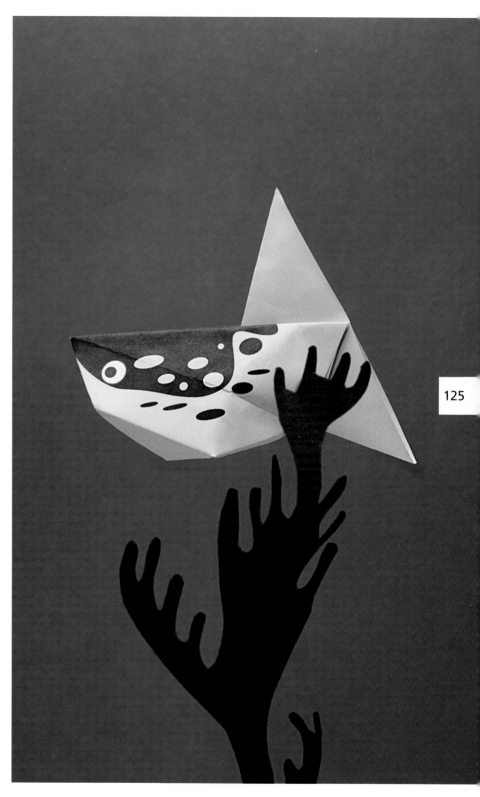

USEFUL INFORMATION

SUPPLIERS

Origami paper is available at most good paper stores or online. Try typing "origami paper" into an internet search engine to find a whole range of stores, selling a wide variety of paper, who will send packages directly to your home address. Or please visit first the author's website: www.happyorigamipaper.com

UK

HOBBYCRAFT
www.hobbycraft.co.uk
Stores nationwide
Tel: + 44 (0)330 026 1400

JP-BOOKS
www.jpbooks.co.uk
24–25 Denman Street
London
W1D 7HU
Opening Hours:
Mon–Sat: 10:30–19:00,
Sun: 11:00–17:00
Tel: + 44 (0)20 7839 4839
Email: info@jpbooks.co.uk

JAPAN CENTRE
www.japancentre.com
19 Shaftesbury Avenue
London
W1D 7ED
Opening Hours:
Mon–Sat: 10:00–21:00
Sun: 11:00–19:00
Email: bookshop@japancentre.com

THE JAPANESE SHOP
www.thejapaneseshop.co.uk
Tel: + 44(0)1423 876 320
Email: info@thejapaneseshop.co.uk

US

MICHAELS STORES
www.michaels.com
Stores nationwide
Tel: 1-800-MICHAELS
(1-800-642-4235)

Amazon.com
Search for "ORIGAMI PAPER"

eBay USA
Search for "ORIGAMI PAPER"

HAKUBUNDO
www.hakubundo.com

CANADA

DESERRES
www.deserres.ca
Tel: + 1-800-363-0318

FRANCE

CULTURE JAPON S.A.S.
www.boutiqueculturejapon.fr
Store in Maison du la Culture du Japon
101 Bis.quai Branly 75015,
Paris
Tel: + 33 (0)1 45 79 02 00
Fax: + 33 (0)1 45 79 02 09
Email: culturejpt@wanadoo.fr

USEFUL WEBSITES

ORIGAMI USA www.origami-usa.org

BRITISH ORIGAMI SOCIETY www.britishorigami.info

NIPPON ORIGAMI ASSOCIATION www.origami-noa.jp

HIROAKI TAKAI "ORIGAMI kyoshitsu" (Japanese only)

KAMIKEY ORIGAMI www.playithub.com

ORIGAMI INSTRUCTIONS www.origami-instructions.com

FURTHER READING

ORIGAMI FOR CHILDREN by Mari Ono and Roshin Ono (CICO Books)

WILD & WONDERFUL ORIGAMI by Mari Ono and Roshin Ono (CICO Books)

ORIGAMI FARM by Mari Ono (CICO Books)

NIHON NO ORIGAMI JITEN (*Dictionary of Japanese Origami*) by Makoto Yamaguchi (Natsume K.K)

INDEX

A
Angel Fish 120

B
Beetle, Japanese Rhinoceros 60
Birds
    Chicken 90
    Duck 82
    Parakeet 100
    Parrot 102
    Peacock 66
    Pigeon 64
Blowfish 124
Bugs
    Cicada 50
    Japanese Rhinoceros Beetle 60
    Ladybug 48
    Snail 62

C
Cats
    Himalayan 24
    Kitten 38
    Persian 28
    Tabby 32
Chicken 90
Cicada 50
Crab, Hermit 116

D
Dachshund 16
Dog 10

Dogs
    Dachshund 16
    Dog 10
    Puppy 34
    Scottish Terrier 20
    Sheepdog 12
Duck 82

E
Edo period 7

F
Ferret 86
Folds
    sikaku ori 7
    sankaku ori 7
    zabuton ori 7
    tako ori 7
Frog 52
furoshiki 7

G
Goldfish 42

H
Hamster 40
Hedgehog 54
Heian period 7
Hermit Crab 116
Himalayan Cat 24
Hopping Rabbit 78
Horse 94
History of *origami* 7

J
Japanese Rhinoceros Beetle 60

K
Kitten 38

L
Ladybug 48
Lizard 112

M
Monkey 104
Mouse 56
Muromachi era 7

O
omotenashi 7

P
Parakeet 100
Parrot 102
Peacock 66
Persian Cat 28
Pig 70
Pigeon 64
Puppy 34

R
Rabbit 74
Rabbit, Hopping 78
Reptiles
    Lizard 112
    Snake 108

S
Scottish Terrier 20
Sheepdog 12
Snail 62
Snake 108

T
Tabby Cat 32
tenugui 7
Terrier, Scottish 20

W
Water-based animals
    Angel Fish 120
    Blowfish 124
    Frog 52
    Goldfish 42
    Hermit Crab 116
Wrapping culture 7

ACKNOWEDGMENTS

First of all, I would like to thank all the readers who purchased and took an interest in this book.

This adorable book was born out of the cooperation of my great friends. My biggest thanks go to Robin Gurdon. As the editor of my *origami* books, he has always instructed and illustrated superb ideas and literature to make for a better understanding of the projects.

My great thanks go to the photographer Geoff Dann. His ability to withstand long hours and many photoshoots during the making of the models, along with his decisive coordination during the shoot, is much appreciated and admired. In addition to his skill as a photographer, Geoff has also emotionally supported all the staff during the production.

Additionally, with the help of my husband, Takumasa Ono (designer of all the *origami* papers) and Trina Dalziel (photoshoot coordinator), this book has become flushed with love and care that is attractive to all readers. From the bottom of my heart, I sincerely appreciate all the help and care that I received during its production.

Finally, thanks also to Cindy Richards and Pete Jorgensen of Cico Books; Midori Christensen and Roshin Ono for helping with the translation of my manuscripts; and all others who were involved in this publication.